Find Your Tribe

Building Deep Community In A
Lonely World

*(A Real Life Guide To Juvenile Arthritis From
People Who Get It)*

Allen Reinke

Published By **Bengion Cosalas**

Allen Reinke

All Rights Reserved

Find Your Tribe: Building Deep Community In A Lonely World (A Real Life Guide To Juvenile Arthritis From People Who Get It)

ISBN 978-1-77485-703-8

No part of this guidebook shall be reproduced in any form without permission in writing from the publisher except in the case of brief quotations embodied in critical articles or reviews.

Legal & Disclaimer

The information contained in this ebook is not designed to replace or take the place of any form of medicine or professional medical advice. The information in this ebook has been provided for educational & entertainment purposes only.

The information contained in this book has been compiled from sources deemed reliable, and it is accurate to the best of the Author's knowledge; however, the Author cannot guarantee its accuracy and validity and cannot be held liable for any errors or omissions. Changes are periodically made to this book. You must consult your doctor or get professional medical advice before using any of the suggested remedies, techniques, or information in this book.

Upon using the information contained in this book, you agree to hold harmless the Author from and against any damages, costs, and expenses, including any legal fees potentially resulting from the application of any of the information provided by this guide. This disclaimer applies to any damages or injury caused by the use and application, whether directly or indirectly, of any advice or information presented, whether for breach of contract, tort, negligence, personal injury, criminal intent, or under any other cause of action.

You agree to accept all risks of using the information presented inside this book. You need to consult a professional medical practitioner in order to ensure you are both able and healthy enough to participate in this program.

Table Of Contents

Chapter 1: The Dumps _____ 1

Chapter 2: The Jerks _____ 20

Chapter 3: A Potential New-Friend-Friend Flinging _____ 41

Chapter 4: Building The Courage _____ 83

Chapter 5: What To Do To Be A Better Friend _____ 124

Chapter 6: The Priority Game _____ 160

Chapter 7: E For Effort _____ 166

Chapter 8: The Treasures Of Life _____ 171

Chapter 9: #Tribeworld _____ 177

Chapter 10: The Right Time Now _____ 181

Chapter 1: The Dumps

I can imagine myself sitting in an amazing loft with exposed bricks and cathedral ceilings in Manhattan's Flatiron and Gramercy areas of Manhattan.

I'm looking at my floor-to ceiling glass windows, which overlook Central Park (This is not physically or geographically feasible within Manhattan's Flatiron or Gramercy areas of Manhattan But I do not really care. I want it all.).

I'm sipping a glass of wine while receiving a special filet by my genetically gifted cheek-chiseled, light brown-eyed Italian living-in cook.

I'm occupied with tending to the different companies I've started. Perhaps I'm the CEO of the one, or perhaps I've assigned that position to someone who has more experience in that position, to ensure that I don't have to think about enjoyable aspects.

When I'm not in my beautiful home in New York City, being pampered by my Chiseled-Jawed-Light-Brown-Eyed-Italian-Chef, I'm traveling the world.

I'm immersed in different culture, meeting people from different countries and taking lessons through their stories.

I am a believer in a double bottom line: my companies and the employees who are employed by them are committed to doing their best by doing well.

It's all very realistic, except the one issue. Whatever wealth I become, I'll be drinking Modelo from the can. You can get her out of being shack but you cannot make the break away from her.

It is possible to live a life that I want. It's just a matter of doing each day something that brings me to a higher level. By inch by inch I'll strive to achieve this goal and live my life the way I want it to be.

There's one thing left out. It's the one that nobody speaks about.

Yes that persistence, hard work and education are important elements that I must have, but I cannot enjoy this or any other worth striving towards regardless of how hard I try or persist if I have shitty friends or if I'm a snarky friend.

Attending Creators Unconference and then unexpectedly staying in the same house with them for couple of months, and the decision to think about my relationships, came in a very strange moment within my own life. "Real living" was staring me in the eye like an annoying older sibling. And the initial two years following college were not easy. I was rejected from every job interview I attended in the event that I been able to get an interview at all. It was a quick process of becoming aware of what I was like professionally as well as personally. "Ready to go, I'm here to help," screamed the harsh reality that I'd been trying for all my life to escape.

Then, I heard a phrase that I didn't realize I required to be hearing: "You are as good as the average of your five closest friends that you have." In a flash I learned that your close friends can unknowingly influence your life and work. The other fact that has brought me to a screeching stop, one that's very uncomfortable to discuss is that what you think you're like as an individual is directly reflected in the people you surround yourself with. Although you might think that you don't have an impact on the relationships you have with others, it's bound to find yourself in the wrong place throughout your life. If you're not aware of your part in it, you're going to be surrounded by snobby acquaintances, and this is likely to manifest as unhappy throughout your life. While those whom I decided to leave had to be eliminated from my world, they also were occasions to reflect on my own actions which in turn sparked self-awareness. Do a thorough glance at your reflection before and after this process. In fact, don't ever stop. Although a brutal and honest resolution may be needed however, it's not an excuse to blame and resentments or block personal growth or advancement.

The chapter has been through many revisions. When I first wrote it I detailed the different behavior in my friends that caused me to end my relationship with them and created fake characters to portray them. However, to claim that an individual's behaviour on its own could result in a breakup or lead to my own breakup, is simply absurd. This is not how I felt about my breakups but I wanted to create specific examples of what to look for in a charming acquaintance, and I believed that simplicity, in this instance was the most effective way to describe it. I had sacrificed authenticity in favor of simplicity, and I was mistaken. The concept isn't easy to grasp.

So I thought I'm gonna I'm going to fuck it. I deleted the entire chapter, and began with the beginning, creating it more authentic and less jarring. What a blast for you.

Certain behaviors in relationships that can cause negative feelings and, therefore, deserve to be ended. Sometimes there's a feeling, an instinctive, guttural itching that tells you that something is going on in your relationship isn't functioning.

When I began the next chapter of my existence, I was aware that I could not do it all on my own. I knew that if were to pursue goals that were difficult to do, like starting new companies I would require a group of sexy people around me. Someone I could trust and who I could trust.

I would like to surround myself with people with the same desires objectives as well as values and interests. Someone who shares my goals for me and in me as well as someone whose goals and visions I am able to communicate with them. I made an unwise decision and it has affected my entire life manner that I really needed and will always require.

"Going on your own," has been given an overly romanticized idea of power. It's bullshit. Absolute and total bullshit. We're not living in the myths that surrounded King Arthur and those of us who try to tie goals together into tangible achievements, aren't knights with shining armor. In our moments of success an entire tribe of badasses may have has helped us reach our goals. The greatest part of this is that you can choose the badasses that surround you. If they're not willing to assist you in moving forward you can leave. Exit is at the back. Always remembering reciprocity, difficult decisions must be made.

Finding out who you really are can be an emotional flow of confidence that is accompanied by debilitating self-doubt. On one side, it is wonderful to be rooted in who you truly are, regardless of the tangled circumstances that brought you to where you are today. However the circumstances that led you to where you are today in the first place, well, they were extremely tense and cause you to question every decision. My failures and the rejections I faced in the years following college (and still have) shed light on the things that attracted me to my friends at the time and the thing that attracted them to me is my inauthenticity. I wasn't myself and didn't be aware of that I was.

Being aware of your inner self will help you to recognize your emotions and how they are related with your relationship. I didn't possess this knowledge until recently. The light bulb came on at the time of the conference at which I first came across Miki Agrawal. I suspected there was something missing, but could not put my finger on it. But then I knew. Then everything changed. I was a grizzly hibernating that woke up and was ready for breakfast.

It could be that all of this manifested in my relationships. If I wasn't me then it's no wonder that my relationships were not functioning. It's no wonder I was attracted to people who weren't a good match for me. I was not the ideal fit for me.

While it's not right to place all the blame on others but it's also wrong to take it all in.

I ended my relationship with those who were extremely critical of me, who had repeatedly deceived me trying to outdo me, snarked constantly or demanded more of me than I allowed them to demand of them. Things like constant delays and snarkiness or having different values were the final straws. And most important was that, in situations of crisis I did not feel that I was able to count on them. Maybe it was due to the fact that they didn't believe they could trust me.

The most crucial aspect in this exercise is self-reflection. However, it's also crucial to identify the behavior of others that could harm you. Look at yourself. What can your actions be taken to improve your friendship more enjoyable? If they're not doing their part, the relationship needs to be ended. It's fine. It's acceptable that you don't want to be friends with somebody who you would not like to be with. It's important to learn from it, improve from it, becoming an even better friend and better person. Look for those who will make it a little more easy for you, and your life and work will prosper.

This is the last piece of the pursuit-of-a-great-career puzzle. Hard work. Perseverance. Education. Wonderful friends.

Who Should Dump

I've admitted that it's not easy. As I've said before in the beginning of the chapter I listed ways to get rid of them and presented them as fake characters that somewhat resembled people from my personal life. This was a mistake; assigning one characteristic to a specific individual implied that the singular behaviour was a reason to break up. It implied that I didn't need to be accountable for my actions and falsely described my experience in breakups as simple and straightforward choices. All of that was not real. There was nothing easy or straightforward however it was worth it.

The decision to leave is an individual decision. You might realize that your relationship isn't working , but not fully comprehending why at first. Take a list of all your friends and then look over your relationships. What do you contribute to these relationships? What needs are being fulfilled and what needs aren't being met, for you and your family members? There are certain things like gossip, lying and unhealthful competition that are easy to recognize and get rid of However, there are many other things that are highly subjective. This is where being aware of your emotional needs, especially as they are related to your relationships is essential to be aware of. What do you require to be missing? Have you said this in your desire? What do you haven't you given to satisfy it? If you've never said it out loud, what's holding you from doing so? If you're experiencing something that is that is holding you back Your gut instinct is usually correct.

Your intuition is your subconscious mind making notes fast enough in order for the conscious brain to get caught the pace (5). In a prior relationship, after being involved for about a year and half, my needs for emotional fulfillment were not being fulfilled, but I hadn't discussed it. My instinct told me when I did and did, it would trigger an instant bolt of lightning towards the exit. I realized I was being silly, and then brought up the thing I thought was lacking. I was correct after all and right to the door, he ran. If that occurs in any relationship, whether platonic or romantic take it as an opportunity. Be clear about your requirements and listen to theirs. However, regardless there are times when you're not the right match.

A Table that is empty Table

"Bringing something new to the table" or the ability to provide something other people don't all want. It's what distinguishes us. It is what gives us a goal. There is something you can give me that I do not own. The need for yin as well as Yang is evolutionary. You set an oven to fry the salmon, while I take the fish. You clean the fields for crop production while I look after the horses who will plough the fields. The fact that we rely on each other is what makes the world go round. Sometimes, neither of us can bring anything on the plate. We're both able to light a fire, however, neither of us is able to catch an eel. We can both use the plow but we don't know how to take care of the horses. Sometimes the table appears empty. As a group, we're not matches. We're not a good fit. We're both yin. an empty table, bodies ill-nourished as well as our horse dead.

Our friendships may result in a empty table as neither one of us has something to offer to the other. It is a way to keep the relationship in a deadlock, never changing, growing or helping any or the other. It's difficult to identify these types of friendships. The empty tables were the cause of several breakups in my life. It took me a long time to realize what was going on, and to realize that we were unfit to be best friends, at least not for the rest of my life.

We had lots of fun, and we gathered humorous and often embarrassing tales. The nights were spent discussing our futures and shared heartbreaks, sharing goals, but completely different in relation to friendship, rendering them completely insanity. The realization was difficult at the time but it's a fact that is worth it today.

The ones who were rude Good riddance. However, the ones who are empty are more difficult to let go. None of you are good people, or even committed any wrongdoing. Together, you're average. There's no way to make each other better.

You aren't able to fill an need in them or they are in you.

Perhaps, this kind of relationship is as harmful as negative ones. This type of friendship doesn't cause emotional trauma in the same as a loss of trust would but it will maintain a stagnation. Complacency breeds more complacency in your professional and personal lives. I don't want my life to be in a solitary space I'd prefer a table full of food and a gathering that is accompanied by mutual respect and understanding that one is meeting the needs of others through our collective efforts to fulfill them.

If you're feeling as if your table is bare It's because you and your companion, together, aren't doing each other any favors. Being in a relationship which does neither anything good stops each of you from becoming the yin of someone else. It doesn't have to be bad in order to be bad. Since empty is more damaging than being bad.

Stop the Hate

The world is laughing along with your Twitter battle.

I've never felt being a snob than when I realized that someone I've had an unresolved grudge has long since forgotten about it. There's just not enough time in the day , as you are, therefore don't spend all of it thinking about people that aren't thinking about you.

The school I attended in high school was, without the need of a better term called a bully, ran a variety of attacks, from yelling names and insulting phrases in the hallway to putting scathing notecards in my lockers, to chasing me down the highway once we began driving. She was an expert at her trade. In my weak, 15-year-old still learning "piss off the h8rs" attitude I let it impact me. Big time. It affected other relationships too, from my most trusted acquaintances to parents. The saga filtered into every nook and crevice of my existence. She even made an army of soldiers, who for a couple of years, selected me as their practice target. I'm not sure they knew the cause they were supporting.

Female bullying is different from male bullying. While boys fight with fists, girls are fighting by using their words and exclusion. Some years of this and I grew an encasement, gradually becoming less interested in their petty jousting, but not completely.

In a totally unexpected plot twist, one that nobody anticipated and not or her troops, she apologised in my senior year. We were all in the theatre department in the same department and, just before curtain time at the beginning of our final show she apologized, saying that she thought, "We could have been friends." I was a bit older and a bit more mature, at least. I mistakenly believed that my growing indestructible skin for wisdom, however, I was completely unprepared in defending myself. Still scolded by many years of torture and stunned by the shocking storyline of my high school story that I believed I was done, I replied by saying something along the lines of, "It's okay."

My first reaction was to say that she had a bullshit story about her apology. I wasn't convinced by her. It was like it was too small, and too late. After school the next day, I decided to visit her at her locker, while she put her textbooks in her backpack. I wanted to ask her with a simple question "Why?" "Why had this happened?" "Why did it start in the first place?"

"I believe that I've just thought that you were against me, and that you believed that I was the reason to dislike me," she said.

In the end, my first thought was to say that I was a"bullshit. When I didn't leave you notebooks or notes inside your bag, or yelled insults at you. Or even drove you off the road, I wanted to shout in incredulity.

However, I began to think about the words she used. As I thought about it, the more I understood the meaning behind her words. She believed that I was a hater of her. She believed that she was acting in the first place. The past four years were to protect her appearance? Was it a game of power caused by anxiety? It was a response to something else happening in her life. She took back the control of something which made her feel like she was out of control.

It was like a heavy weight lift off me with my newfound wisdom. I should have talked to her and demanded her to stop, and told her that she was harming me. This would have stopped everything. If she had known the way she was working and was aware of it, she wouldn't have carried on. Perhaps it would have. What do you think? The only thing I can say is that hate was not the solution or even holding grudges certainly wasn't the solution. Hate does no one good. It perpetuates the cycle of pain making it more difficult to overcome. Letting go of her , and the things she did was the best solution.

Takeaways

1. The hard work, perseverance and education are essential to achieving your career goals But the missing piece is to surround yourself with amazing people.

2. Every aspect of your life could be changed by the right words spoken from the person at the right location. Be open to the possibility of change whenever they appear.

3. Grudges are reserved for losers.

4. Be kind to everyone, particularly the people who aren't nice to you, because they might require it the most.

5. The person you choose to break up with is a matter of opinion and you may not know, but when you're in the position of knowing you're in the know, you'll be able to tell.

6. Don't allow your body to become hungry and your horses dying. Don't leave the table to be empty. Find the yin in your yin and eat at the table that you set for one another.

7. Never hold grudges. You're just wasting your time.

Chapter 2: The Jerks

"UNAPOLOGETIC" is my favorite Word within the English language.

My most favorite phrase that I use in French is "parapluie." It's a French word that means umbrella, and it is funny when spoken with a strong French accent.

Ask someone French person to speak French and then watch them hate you.

My personal favorite term that I use Italian is "basta" because it is a reference to "stop" and "enough," but it is a good word to use in many different situations such as when you're angry, or you've had a bad meal.

When I was on an entire semester in Italy I came up with an -may I say fantastic idea of naming an Italian eatery Basta Pasta. It rhymes, and there's no pasta enough!

When I returned home to New York, I learned that there was an establishment called Basta Pasta, but the food featured an Asian and Italian mix.

This isn't logical. I'm disgusted, all about it. Italian people are very specific regarding their meals. At gelato stores, it's standard to get two flavors, but they need the two to work well. I've been banned from a gelato establishment due to requesting a mix that the owner of the shop believed was not good. I'm not sure that they'd be thrilled to find someone who paired your food and drinks with Asian food. While I'm not as proficient in Asian culture like I am in Italian I can imagine that they'd feel exactly the same. Both are delicious in their own right however not as well together.

I must admit, I was angry about it. Still am. I'll probably never be able to get over it.

But I digress. Basta and return to the topic. "Unapologetic" has a slickness to it, which affirms its message it makes you feel powerful in the moment it's uttered from your mouth. It's not necessary to defend it, since it stands for its own sake. It has an innate force that makes making your own voice much more easy.

Do it in a loud voice and you'll be able to see what I'm talking about.

I am unapologetic. I'm not apologetic for the decision to dump people I love who deserve to be thrown out. I'm not ashamed of leaving their lives without warning or formal discussion or apology.

That's what I'm trying tell you is that I ghosted.

What was it that I was holding onto I was holding on to? I considered this before taking my final decision about leaving. My conclusion was: Nothing. I'm holding onto nothing. The friendships were not satisfying. There were a few individuals who were not good for me. From constant competition with each other, gossiping and lying as well as the desire to spend the most time with my ex-partner rather than with me, to being betrayed and passive aggressively disregard for others, some people simply had to go. Even through my brief absence from friends and second-guessing my decision, I've never regretted the decisions I made. Because during the period of loneliness and isolation of this experience I was conscious that I did not want to be a shite about myself or my friendships. This chapter isn't as in depth than the other ones since toxicity is straightforward. Do you find someone who makes you feel bad about you often? Don't bother them. Toxicity is characterized by its behaviors. In the event that being known as a sh*thead has become something you do regularly you're familiar with the procedure. I've been through a few of them and putting them behind me was a great feeling. I felt rejuvenated, inspired in my pursuits and more confident in my abilities when I made new friends who supported each other.

My Epic Speeches that I've Designed Just in case

Ghosting these particular acquaintances was the best idea I've ever had. It was refreshing. However, it left me feeling empty, in the place where an epic speech about breaking up could be.

Of course I spent the next couple of weeks thinking about the possibilities of what I might have done.

There was a person for who I spent a lot of my precious shower time making incredible speeches, shower time which could be used to think about the possibility of winning the lottery performing the front of an imagined sold-out arena of fans who are awed or fantasizing over Paul Rudd laughing at my jokes. (Paul Rudd is my love of my life, and I hope that one day you will meet him and love me. He might even think that I'm funny. You'll see. It'll happen.)

There was an ex-boyfriend who I was too thinking about after the breakup. Most of the time, I was angry at myself for having dated him at all in the first place. The lies he spun kept growing and eventually I got enough.

I've included him in a book on friends since we were wrongly, friends after the breakup that, in retrospect, was extremely regrettable. I don't like hindsight. That bitch is always right , and she is aware of that. The friendship we maintained post-breakup was due to a sense of relationship of affection we couldn't let go of up. Due to this, and the apparent growing of our emotional bond that was a result of the "we're bound to become the best friends for life" constructed narrative breaking up with friends was more difficult to deal with than the romance one. And the emotional connection I didn't yet realize was false led me to remain with the friendship for longer than I ought to have.

I wanted to be Julia Roberts and Dermot Mulroney in My Best Friend's Wedding (6). After a time before they realized that they could be more successful as friends , and then became great friends.

The scene where Julia is trying to gain back Dermot isn't relevant in this instance.

Don't attempt to become close to your ex. We're not within My Best Friend's Wedding, and we don't get friends with our ex-partners.

We're exes with reasons. Take a lesson from the mistakes I made.

In the end, following a hurtful betrayal and being implicated in a couple of more lies I walked away from his sexy ego again, this time for the second time. First time around, more than one year ago I walked away from the man as my lover. the second time, I tossed the guy as a friend. Since then, I've not seen him.

In the initial few weeks after the break-up (the first one was as two of us) I imagined returning to him and reciting everything I could have said if I had not been ghosted.

But, I didn't completely make up my mind about him. I discovered yet another one, and when I did, we had a an extremely brief text message exchange that read like this:

"You're a fucking liar."

"Excuse me?"

"Fuck off."

It was that simple. Then I thought about how the conversation would unfold should I meet him once more, and the entire story that surrounded it.

I imagined we'd be with a group of our friends who were mutual when someone asked about what transpired to us, saying that we were "So well-liked." They would murmur, "She's a bitch," in his mouth since that's what he'd do. In the meantime the man was already dating a new person. The truth is I knew her name and we were always told that we were alike.

I answer the author's "Bitch," with this:

There's something you're always able to overlook about me. In situations like this, can be extremely useful.

It's easy to forget that I'm also an author. and that I'm part of an amazing family of writers. Do you know the meaning of that? This means I am able to create my own words to taste. They can be made to taste exactly like whatever I want them to.

I could transform them into a warm, chocolate-chip cookie, and sweet tea. You could also make them taste like heroin, flowing into your bloodstream for the first time and filling you with life-giving liquids.

It is also possible to make them taste like an iron blade cutting the spinal cord. It's just several seconds so it's time to...

Bake.

If I'm feeling like tasting iron, I can break you limb from leg in one swift swipe.

Whoever claimed that "sticks and stones may cause me to break bones, but words will never harm me" was full of the shit. At least, he's never been scolded by a wordsmith or ex-boyfriends who were witty.

Actually, I believed I was in need of you. For a brief time of weakness truly believed that I required you. But when you didn't appear I realized that, I didn't needed you, but I didn't even want you.

I'm not looking for an oath-breaker, a lie or the glass-half-empty personification. When I finally came to this realization I felt like Atlas. That statue of the man who holds the globe around one side of his neck? It was like I was finally handing the globe on to unassuming schmuck.

This poor, innocent person, of course is Tory who I feel very sorry for. Because, well, she's unsuspecting. She's a lovely adorable girl. She probably believes you're a nice, adorable guy that's an end of the road but somewhat lovable.

Many people have stated that she's like me which isn't a good thing. It's not just for me. For me it's a symphony combining comedy and poetry. It's as the scenario if

Walt Whitman came back from the dead and created films together with Will Ferrell. (Actually it's an idea for an idea for a script. If you were Mr. Ferrell, what do you think? I would love it me if you made this.)

I am so sorry for I am sorry for. Your insecurity is evident through the actions of people who surround you. You manipulate, profit of, and betray people you love. I would like to never meet you again.

I wish that others around you realize that your charming and humorous facade isn't really the person you are. you're really unsecure, manipulative, and simply a vulgar person.

Then, I would conclude the show with a variation that sounded like "fuck off!" which eventually will cause a person in the audience to begin with a slow clap since they've realized just that he is a complete idiot he truly is and how much they appreciate me sharing it with them.

Wow!! It took me several weeks to think of it. After that, I was past it. I didn't even care that I would ever see him again. It was an utter waste of shower time.

After a couple of weeks of consuming calories through the overly indulgence of frozen ice cream I was no longer feeling the need to deliver this speech any more. It was a transition from being obsessed about our relationship throughout the entire time--the romantic aspects as well as the platonic aspects--to being completely uninterested in his existence.

It's like straight from One Tree Hill, right? I am sure. It's great. (I've been watching One Tree Hill on Netflix and, now since I'm no longer an unhappy teenager, it's a totally distinct experience.)

Let your hand up if you have a similarly ridiculous speech you've prepared in honor of an old friend. If you had an opportunity to make it did you? No, of course not. Because your life isn't an soap-opera! Your life isn't One Tree Hill, as it is as you'd like to think it is. It's also because it would be silly to actually deliver an address like this.

This kind of therapy is far cost-effective in terms of cash and time. I do it for an act of healing and in private. Although yelling at someone at the time feels good however, you'll regret it when you wake up. That's another problem to be obsessed over , and it's not worth the effort. Saying snarky things about ex-friends or boys/girlfriends isn't something I'd like to be famous for launching. However, I am determined to be the type of person who can successfully begin with a slow clap. One next day I'll prove the recipient of this feat.

The Effects Residual of Ghosting

Ghosting, as used in the context of Friendshit is not the current pop-culture term to refer to a date who has never responded to your messages It is more of "just going away." It's the best method to break up a friendship and I would highly recommend it. However, it could have lasting consequences. It may, depending on the situation result in the feeling of a gap that will be filled by an epic speech you'll never deliver.

Though I'm inclined to believe "closure" is not a good idea but there's an element of truth for being the last word. And in the absence of words it can be difficult to feel an unfulfilling feeling that you may attempt to cover by addressing your own personal flaws If you allow yourself to.

One of the emotional weaknesses that ghosting can exacerbate is obsession. As with all things that are negative for your health it's addictive.

Obsession for me, looks like pain, anxiety and a waste of calories from extravagant ice cream sundaes and the wasted time of showering with totally ridiculous, but impressive speeches that are never heard.

I am on the obsessive cycle following any breaking up or hurtful event. I am in mattress, undressed (I'm generally not dressed when I'm on my own since why wouldn't I?). I feel awful at myself for my world-wide problems , and I look at my phone in hope that someone will call me. If it seems ridiculous, it's because it's extremely embarrassing.

Take a look away with your judge-y eyes.

It's true that I'm not exactly the only person to have been through it, but that doesn't mean that it's a good thing. Even if we're all doing it, this doesn't mean it's any less dangerous. The addicts that are all around us should band together. My name is Allison.

The thing is that obsession can be life-threatening, career-threatening and good vibes ruining. If you don't learn to use it to benefit over the long term learning from your experience and then move on and be a better person and friend Put obsession into the blender, and then turn to self-awareness.

Being aware of who you're and being able to identify your flaws and strengths helps you be more in touch with people who are of high quality and become a better person, and make better choices in your professional and personal life and is the basis for the decisions you make throughout the course in your lifetime.

You can therefore spend your hours focusing on the wrong things or utilize your energy to improve your self-awareness. the most valuable asset that a person could ever have.

At one point, I allowed myself to fall into dark places , without being able to learn from them. I let my obsession, as well as the pain of friendships broken and love lost overtake my life. What you see on sitcoms like a person who is who is eating a lot while sitting in a towel that is soaking because they had to shower but it was a lot of effort and amount of energy and they're crying out in a rage while mascara runs across her face. That shit is real. Sure, it's hilarious when you see an actor or actress perform the same thing. In real life, it's not quite so funny. However, it is still entertaining.

Now, I still obsess. But I obsess with more intelligence.

I'm able to focus on my smarter habits by accepting that I am feeling it without feeling guilt. The more you battle it and the more you sink. Obsession is like quicksand however, it's Indiana Jones and you're too intelligent to be a fool.

Let yourself feel it. Do some powerful speech in your shower and consume as many extravagant ice cream cones as you can. Instead of letting your hurt take over you, learn from it, and leverage it into increasing self-awareness. Then allow it to assist you be a better friend and to make new friends.

You can be a sitcom for a short for a while, then stand up and get out of bed and put on lipstick and get back to work. Sometimes, I skip my lipstick application.

Begin by defriending. Digitally, by that I mean. It's impossible to make it happen offline until it takes place online. You're only putting yourself in danger by checking their Facebook page on a daily basis. Therefore, don't allow yourself to choose.

Obsessing on being smarter is being able to hurt yourself and creating a space in which the pain can be only brief and effective. It's not possible to be temporary or productive if these stories are popping on your newsfeed each day.

Delete, unfriend, unfollow.

Find ways to be more.

Removing friends, no matter whether it's your decision isn't an easy task. There's a period of time that you've never seen anyone you've never met before. Be sure to trust your instincts and the reasons for leaving from the beginning. You'll emerge from the other end feeling more positive and more confident than you ever imagined you could be.

Why aren't People Punching the Jerks In The Face Anymore?

Moving away is probably how you learned to manage tension. But what about being angry and being a fighter for yourself?

I'm not a fan of striking people. Most of the time , I'm in the position of preaching the "just leave" approach, but at times I'd like to hit the jerks directly in the face.

I'd like to be able to walk out of their lives without having to give them a reason. I would like be able to say to them: get off and to tell them the fact that they're not important to me as a person who's negatively impacted my life, that getting rid of them was the most beneficial thing I could do for myself I believe that my life will be more enjoyable without them, and that they're sloppy and I don't want them. Yes, we all feel these emotions that are fueled by anger and simply being human. But what is more painful than a fist to a kisser? Are you ready to see this plot twist? Vulnerability.

Being vulnerable to those who have hurt you is extremely powerful. For those who hurt you, it could be an enormous blow in the face. It's unexpected, reflective and truly shows determination.

This is your opportunity to show your unapologetic side.

Punch the jabs in the face literally.

Being insecure is frightening.

Imagine listening to something like: "You hurt me. Your actions were harmful to me. I was irritated for several some time, and although I am feeling great and am moving on but the impact your actions caused me were negative."

It is referred to as a knockout.

Letting myself be vulnerable has opened up a number of opportunities for me. It's shown the world that there's far more positive people than people who are bad, that the majority of people look for vulnerability in others to determine if it's acceptable to be vulnerable and that people react to vulnerability more strongly than any other thing.

Let Go of the Grudges

As I stated in Chapter 1 of this book, There will always be those who you're glad to let go. You'll be hurt by them , and eventually you'll arrive at a point when you're willing to release them completely. The moment will come release any anger.

Every single person on the planet has their own daily struggles and fights. It doesn't mean that we shouldn't keep them out of our lives, but it does mean we need to understand and be grateful for the struggles of others.

Give them forgiveness. Then let them go.

It's okay to let go and to decide whether or not you wish to have them to be in your lives. But you're not permitted to in a state of mindless anger as if you're Montagues as well as the Capulets. Do better than fictional characters who died tragically. Simply be better.

Takeaways

1. Be unapologetic.

2. The relationships that are toxic are those you need to eliminate first. From manipulators to liars as well as the jealous and overly competitive, look for these traits on the spot and anyone else who is regularly displaying them.

3. Writing an epic speech about your breakup can be the most relaxing thing to do although they shouldn't necessarily be seen. You can get my Epic Breakup Speech template at allisoneconway.com/friendshitbonuses!

4. Obsession, just like everything else that are harmful, can be addictive. Removing yourself from an unhealthy relationship is the best choice, however it could have residual results, in the form of obsessiveness. Learn to harness it , and be more aware of your obsession. It can be transformed into self-awareness by studying it and then letting it go.

5. If walking away from the situation doesn't work, hit the jerk in the face, literally. Hit them directly in the face, showing genuine vulnerability, as I would do with the bully in my High School.

6. Grudges are only for losers.

Chapter 3: A Potential New-Friend-Friend Flinging

The process of forming a new friendship is so difficult. It's not as easy as regular flirting, where you just lean into, touch an elbow or knee, smile flick your eyes, and then get free drinks. It's not that I have too many experiences with that.

Finding new friends after college seems to be a challenge. Making new friends at work can be a possibility provided that the work environment is conducive to some socializing. This can be difficult to find.

There's no need for parents-created playdates that weren't all that good anyway. Mom once invited the incorrect "Megan." That was an absolute nightmare. So far as I can tell the social norms stop being acceptable once you reach the age of the age of nineteen. Or a decade earlier. Whatever.

I realized that I would have be creative for me to connect with new people, with or without mommy's guidance. And, by the way, Mom please make my flights booked for the working trip scheduled for in the next month. Great, thanks. #adulthood.

How can you connect with people? I was a recent graduate of college. There was no normal 9-5 job in which I could have a social gathering in a workplace. I was also unsure of how people met their friends , if not at these two places.

I quickly realized that I had to become a nerd.

I Got Ballsy: Part 1.

By"bumpsy", I'm talking about the time I went to events on my own and pretend to be extremely outgoing.

This chapter focuses on what I experienced when I went to events, conferences, or events by myself. I have a few tricks in my sleeves that made it easier for me to get there and I'll detail them all.

It all started by attending an appearance at the General Assembly conference in May 2015. It was not just that I met an amazing person and inspiring, she was the type of person I wanted to spend time with and the type of person who would help me become more of a person. She inspired me by her own actions, and displayed a variety of traits I wanted to be around with. I also knew that we could learn and develop from one another.

Now, Frannie and I are business partners and are on the way to creating incredible things together.

A couple of weeks later after a lengthy working session with my new business partner and friend I made at the conference I decided to go out for a drink. It was the first time I had been to a bar for almost a year and I wanted to get drunk. My friends at the time did not feel at all like drinking, and that was frustrating.

It's not much worse than wanting to go out while everyone else is thinking of staying in and getting to bed early. It's not just that you want to stay home and get up early even though everyone else is drinking and having a drink.

Then I thought"fuck it. I'm looking forward to going out and so I'm going for a night out. I used to live within my NYU Building located in The East Village of Manhattan and the area is essentially an undiscovered treasure trove of bar crawls and a plethora of nightlife.

I walked around, searching for a spot with an edgy vibe, one that could be a good idea to go into alone. I was searching for an establishment that didn't be a huddle of people gathered in circles that were too difficult to engage in an exchange of words. I was seeking people of a certain individuals aged between mid- and late-twenties.

The summer in Manhattan is often referred to as "Intern Season" due to the influx of college-aged interns that fill the city, while the rest of us typically leave to head to the Hamptons or another beach area during the weekend. It's very easy to be stuck in the bar with a crowd of interns at this time of the season, and I wanted to stay clear of that as much as I could.

Being hit by a bunch of teens who couldn't grow beards wasn't the way I imagined a great time.

I was required to have armor if I were going to be doing this on my own. I needed a venue which wasn't just a horde of men in suits, because they you'll sigh, even though it's much more enjoyable then talking with girls. When I'm with guys, I only need to engage in flirting. However, girls are a lot more difficult and need a bit more flirting.

I chose a location that seemed to meet my rather loose criteria I went in, bought an alcoholic drink and took a bathroom break, drank my drink to get some liquid courage, then got another drink, and then began looking for other people to speak to.

I was standing on the wall when two women who appeared to be in their mid-twenties came over trying to move out of the way of the guys in the bar. They were drinking a lot shots Fireball shots.

I spent a few minutes listening to their conversations They weren't discussing something weird. That's perfect I thought. They're normal.

I admired one of the ladies' shoes and I was all in.

"Thanks!" She said"Thanks!" and I wanted to know her name. Julie.

Her friend decided to join in on the conversation.

"What?" She asked.

"She told me she liked the shoes I wear," Julie answered.

"Oh Oh, yes I'm telling you that I love them each time you put them on."

I gave the girl I was my name and requested hers. Erin.

I explained to them that I got out of a relationship just a few months prior and that I was looking to meet some guys. They were in agreement. We decided that this wasn't the right place for it So we went to in the East Village in pursuit of hot men, and preferably not interns. Since isn't that what twenty-something girls do?

We then got drunk, and then met a couple of dudes whom we decided not to particularly like, and then continued to drink. I had a fantastic evening with new friends and all since I told one girl that I loved her shoe. Who would have believed that you could get to know chicks in the bar?

It's difficult to converse with strangers, particularly since we're told as kids that talking to strangers can be risky.

It's not like that we should cease instructing children to not talk with strangers. However, it is important to learn that lesson as adults. Most people are nice and won't try to murder or rob you.

Being in a place of experiencing new things and getting to know different people can be the sole way to experience new things in your life and make new friends (uh duh!). However, just like all of us, this notion makes me shiver. But I don't let that keep myself from trying it. We'll discuss what I do within the next section.

If I had remained in my room, in anxiety of possibly being judged or being viewed as an idiot, I could never have had the chance to meet Julie and Erin or Frannie.

Of course, I've tried this before but not with the same results. I like the "I love your shoes" line often. Girls are awestruck by compliments, and for certain girls, this line works just fine. However, for others, it doesn't work as much.

I signed up for a membership to the Metropolitan Museum of Art at the beginning of summer 2015 due to I firstly love the MET, but also as a way to make use of it to meet new people.

They have a party each summer for members between 21-35 years old They very imaginatively refer to as"the "Young Members Party." (7) I decided to check it out to find out what kind of atmosphere it would be.

Dressed up and looking classy I strolled about looking to mingle and mix.

I saw a woman in the dress which I recognized as being a new Valentino style. In amazement, I asked, "Is your dress Valentino? It's gorgeous. You're gorgeous!" She looked at me with eyes that were dreadful.

She replied, "Yeah, it is thank you." She turned back to walk away. Lady, you're just trying to be kind.

As with the rest of love is a game of numbers. Some people are likely to be nice, while others won't.

Everybody has a form of social anxiety. However, conquering them is a one of the steps to becoming a sexy. I encourage you to get over your fears by confronting them head-on. You may even make new acquaintances from it.

Be a sexy.

Get fearless. Get yourself out of your comfortable zone. I'm asking you to go out on your own this evening and compliment a woman's shoes. It's likely that you won't get to be able to meet your new best friend however that's not the goal.

The point is to do something--anything--that forces you out of your comfort zone, that pushes you to overcome your fears by facing them, something that puts you in a place where you can tell your weaknesses to go fuck themselves.

What do you think of her after complimenting her shoes?

Have you been to networking events and only shared awkward silences as you shake hands as you try to manage your drink and platter of food items as you ask, "What do you do?" a million times?

I've never been able to make a permanent connection with conversations that started at "what are you doing?" It's a conversation one that's a frightener. DOA.

I prefer to start meeting new people believing that they'll be excited to meet people they've never met. Most of the time, they are however, even if they're not, I'm not losing any of my confidence by remaining positive.

Begin by opening with an opener such as a compliment, or an observation. Be sure to keep it positive. It's risky to be negative and you shouldn't start off with a negative attitude.

If it's something you're sure of agreeing on, such as the weather or your displeasure towards Donald Trump, don't bring the subject up. It's a dead-end.

A simple compliment from her is a great way to start. You could also say things like "I've not been here before. It's amazing!" or "The drinks are always amazing here!"

After the opening, jump straight into. Do not talk about small things. Completely.

I contacted Julie as well as Erin by letting them know that I had recently walked separated from a partner and was a bit sad and wanted to have fun and meet new people at least for fun.

They immediately jumped in and they were keen to support me. They wanted me to enjoy a fun night out and were able to relate to my feelings of loneliness and sad following the breakup of a couple recently.

Do not ask "What are you doing?" for the entire first time you meet this person, regardless of whether it is uncomfortable to bring the subject up. It's a question that everyone wants to know when they meet in New York, and I'm immediately disengaged whenever they ask. It's as if people are quick to figure out how much you earn.

In this day and age of freelance work and more and more people stepping away from their "regular" occupation, a lot of people don't know what to do with this question. Furthermore, asking this question to initiate a conversation suggests that you're the only thing important about someone, and suggests you're judging them on the answer they provide.

What one "does" does not define what they're about and this is not a good method to create the creation of a new, meaningful connection.

My personal favorite is "What's the most exciting event that's happening to you?" They will usually appear to look at you like there are two heads since you're probably the only person they've ever asked the question, especially in the first time they meet. But I'm sure your conversation will go on for hours.

If you're not confident enough to ask such an open-ended inquiry straight away You can tell them something about yourself . This could be used as an invitation to them to talk about some of their own personal information.

I shared with Julie along with Erin about my break-up, because I knew being women in their 20s, they would be capable of understanding. I also believed that they might have shared any boyfriend stories or their own.

Being honest about something personal such as feeling vulnerable following an breakup, isn't logical when you're making new acquaintances. Many people hide their vulnerability till they "warm up" to a new acquaintance. However, that's the exact contrary of the way we ought to be doing. Inviting people to come in immediately will show them they can communicate with you from the beginning as well. When people feel that you're reliable and are honest and honest, you're done. Connections are was made.

I Got Ballsy: Part 2.

I was lucky to meet Julie and Erin in this way. Even though that's not the typical way friendships develop It proves everything is possible by putting yourself in situations where something can occur.

It's an excellent way to exercise expanding your comfort zone however in bars, you're looking at the bar in the dark (sometimes literally) in an attempt to meet interesting people. It's time to focus on your. Locations where people share an element similar (a quality or a characteristic you would like to possess or to surround yourself with) is another excellent opportunity to connect with people.

Think about those you would like to have a relationship with? Who are the people that you would like to be? What are your passions? Where do they hang out?
Then, go to those locations.

I want to be as successful as the cool social entrepreneurs I encountered in the General Assembly conference. They meet at meet-ups, conferences fashionable cafes and restaurants in NYC and co-working spaces and many other venues.

They're continuing to learn about their area of expertise through classes online or in person in technology, coding and design, business, as well as a variety of other abilities.

So, I attend events, meet-ups trendy cafes in NYC and co-working spaces. I also take classes in technology, coding design, business, and.

Make a list of the kinds of people you'd like to follow or become friends with and the places they are hanging out. Certain places may not be as evident. Many entrepreneurs are health conscious and so the idea of joining a group tour that visits new restaurants that are healthy in NYC is an excellent option.

You can join fitness clubs such as ClassPass (8) as well as experience various fitness classes in the city. (I've done this, and not only is ClassPass give you access to a variety of gyms, I've also met lots of super awesome people.) They don't pay me to endorse them I simply am in love with them. Keep killing it ClassPass!

Visit Meetup.com (9) for more information and you'll see a range of groups which you can join. There are filters that allow you to sort through groups and plenty of options to pick from, from drinking to happy hours for tech executives, and all between. Start attending every one you can and don't be waiting for someone to tell you they'll join you.

Be yourself and engage with a variety of people. Take a few ounces of confidence if you feel it is suitable for the occasion. A few drinks is fine, but drinking a lot at such events is not the ideal method to create a positive impression.

Except for bar crawls. If so, you should start making shots. You are at your own risk.

There are happy hour groups or hiking groups, and meetings for those who love cats and cat-related videos (probably). There's practically anything you can think of. It's crucial to attend these events without anyone you already have a relationship with.

When you go to a party alone you're required to speak to strangers. If you're with your friend or someone you're comfortable with, you're not more compelled to interact with strangers.

A friend is bringing your familiarity zone. Put yourself in a position where meeting strangers is feasible. Your comfort zone is not a problem.

There are a variety of events and conferences via the Eventbrite app (10). They are fantastic because, as with Creators Unconference, you will not only meet amazing individuals, but learn a lot about the particular industry the conference is targeted at. I gained some great knowledge from the speakers, and also met a business associate all in the same day.

It's not necessary to pay everything but the last 70 dollars, like the fool I was. Many of the events in this app are for free. Let's go out and get super-sexy!

Simply show up

All you need to do is simply show up. It's that easy. By being present, I'm referring to being present. Make conscious decisions to make improvements.

The ball is in your court. Other analogies from sports.

Place yourself in situations that enable you meeting new friends. Simply living your life will not necessarily make it worse, in any way. However, it won't necessarily make it better.

You can go alone in bars and tell people that you are impressed by their footwear You can visit meetup.com to find other targeted groups to join. Or, you can take a class and make friends through attending events and conferences in the city nearest to you as well as in the field you are interested in.

If you aren't in an area where these types of groups or conferences usually take place make an individual group. Begin going to eateries in your neighborhood and invite others to go with you.

Begin to hike and invite friends to join you. It doesn't matter what you do. Do something to result in situations where meeting interesting, new people is likely. Don't do anything that is that's illegal. If you make a mistake, don't blame this author or myself. 'Kay, thanks.

Making your own choices each day is a routine as simple as taking care of your teeth. If you decide to design your own destiny, things begin to happen that in ways you didn't expect to create.

I was at the McDonald's located below my apartment located in my apartment on the Upper East Side of Manhattan after an evening of drinking with college buddies who were visiting. My block also featured a Yogurtland and the Chipotle. It was a very risky block. After I had consumed my traditional drinking Big Mac (a ritual that only began when I lived above the level of a McDonald's and was thankfully over once I relocated) I reached into my ugly bag that was gifted my way by an lady I employed for one time, only to find that my keys were not there. Not surprised by my frequently forgetfulness I reached for on to the shoulder of one of my former college buddies and told him, "We're sleeping in Central Park."

I could tell that he wasn't interested in the conversation, however I decided to stay away from his concerns. We arrived at Central Park, which was just a few minutes away from my house, and then took a walk straight towards Bethesda Fountain.

Bethesda Fountain, one of my favourite spots in the entire city. It was also the place I decided to remain for the remainder of the night.

Intoxicated enough to forget what anybody was thinking, I turned on some music and began dancing as the dancer I was. In my early years I totally forgot that my time at Central Park at 4:00 a.m. I didn't even notice that the man who was homeless and taking money from the fountain was gazing at me; I didn't notice that I couldn't hear the music on my mobile; and I didn't think what the Scandinavian couple who had been watching me for the entire time or the fact that the friend I've been dragging with me not seen me dance before and is probably thinking I'm insane.

I took a break from dancing as if nobody is watching to go into the fountain and assist the homeless man take the wishes of tourists. We soon realized that all the quarters were already gone or, perhaps that most people would just throw in pennies to pay for their wishes. We laughed and said that perhaps their wishes would have more luck when they weren't as cheap about it.

Dante in his own words to me is a war veteran and one of the many unfortunate recipient of an "Dear John," letter along with other tragedies typical of war. Based on my experience of hearing about different war tales, I was expecting to hear something more lengthy. However, once he had told me the basics the man did not stop. Incredulous at his conciseness, I listened to him.

The Scandinavian woman who was watching me dance joined Dante with me and Dante in the fountain. She told me she was awed by seeing me dancing. I was elated, as I had not danced for years I was unable to hear the next thing she said following the fact. I reenter conversations when she talks about her participation in the ALS Ice Bucket Challenge. The challenge was nominated by her friends to take part in it, and thought that swimming under the sprinklers in the fountain was just cold enough. She asked me to dance along with her in her video on Facebook and then jump through the water that was gushing around together. In retrospect, I realize the fact that this is odd but my ego wouldn't refuse.

We talked the rest evening, and promised to stay in contact and visit our respective cities once more. We're still friends through Facebook which is why I will never forget that strange night when I took one of my friends into Central Park, chose to attend, and meet amazing people. The evening could have been a negative one however I chose not to let it happen.

Being present, and being honest to the people around you, or doing something a bit crazy, accepting to be a part of the footage of a stranger's Ice Bucket Challenge video, could and will alter everything.

What's the worst thing that could be the case?

What are the ramifications of going on the limb in this manner? Let's take a look.

It is possible to be rejected. You might be unable to stand up in an unwelcoming corner. You might be viewed with a sneer, like the Valentino lady was looking at me. You might leave the premises without ever speaking to anyone. You could be spending money on events, drinks or memberships that don't make sense for you.

Will you ever be able to live? It's possible, but not likely. Are you likely to be killed or being robbed? It's unlikely. Are you likely to leave with a that is life-threatening or traumatizing? It's probably not.

What's the biggest thing that could occur? Examine the possibilities which could happen and you'll realize they're not a huge issue. If the most that could occur is that you don't meet anyone or aren't accepted, is that really that bad?

The rewards are almost always exceed the risk. You may leave without a dime, or some hurt feelings and your self-esteem a bit damaged. But you can make new friends, amazing connections, self-confidence, and self-awareness, as well as an entirely new perspective on life.

Which side do you want to take the victory?

Begin With Family

If we're happy with it and/or not, it's part of our family. It's impossible to leave them, no regardless of how hard we try. They are our very first family and are genetically trained to be loyal, love you, and come back , no matter how many times you mess up (or even create a book full of F-bombs).

As a mature adult is me, I'm discovering that my family are likely to become my closest family members as my life changes. My brother's older brother recently got married to a girl who I enjoy (what an amazing relief). It has brought me closer my brother, and I have a friend for life in the new wife he has. My younger brother is at college, but is quickly making his own brand of brawny. He's incredibly politically and rant-y. He'll either end up as an activist or politician. God will, it's going to be the former.

Many of our friends will be absent because of a variety of factors but regardless of whether we enjoy this or not our family will remain around for the rest of our lives. Begin to befriend them. It is much less effort than just hating them. It requires a lot of energy to hate them. The reason you should hate your parents is because they are teens who are angsty (been there been there, done that).

There's something that everyone in the World has in Common

I've instructed you to do some weird items in the chapter. I'm not apologizing for telling you to do some crazy activities, but let me tell you a hint that makes the process a bit more enjoyable.

You've probably heard the suggestion "Imagine the audience wearing their underwear" as you prepare to deliver a speech or speak in front of an audience of a lot of people. It's probably the worst advice I've heard.

Seriously, it's terrible. What if the viewers are extremely attractive? This could make it more difficult and distracting. It's not like the audience is wearing their underwear.

Imagine them as a family.

Imagine the crowd or anyone who is too for you to speak to in front of his or her family.

What do all people on earth share in common? A strange family.

You can also use it in your favor.

Imagine any person who is intimidating with their family. Imagine the woman on the first row, trying to keep Uncle Joe from smacking at her college roommates or Aunt Sally not saying to her "go look for a nice guy," suddenly she's human and has been taken off the high-heeled pedestal.

What if the person that you admire most was the one the one who burned the rolls on holiday? Would you consider her to be anything less than perfection? However, she is. She is, and she always has been. Because she's human.

Like you and me the most terrifying people around the globe need to endure the holiday every year. And for those in the world who do not celebrate the holiday of

Thanksgiving, there's a day to celebrate too, where your family's weird behavior is displayed.

Since let's face it, every person on the planet has a bizarre fucking clan.

Doesn't that sound better than thinking about the underwear of those in your closet? Yes, I believe so, goodness.

The Concept That Worked for Me

When I was around fifteen years old My Mom took me to an Chanel trunk show in the mall. The mall wasn't that we would usually shop at however, it was a place that was forty-five minutes away, which had all the fancy shops. I felt that I was required to put on a dress to go there, and felt that I wasn't a part of the community.

This was the first time I attended a fashion event and what I didn't realize at the time was that it wouldn't be the last time I attended. I instantly became obsessed with fashion and Chanel.

While I could not pay for anything I saw the day before, and I even today but I was able to admire clothing and the imagination and workmanship of their designers. I declared fashion my life's passion and started planning my entire life around pursuing working in the field of fashion editorial.

When I was in my senior year of the college I attended, and was looking for internships and positions for magazines or any position within the industry of fashion. I submitted a plethora of cover letters, resumes and emails that seemed like asking (because it was) to be thrown into the darkness which is Internet.

Then, a few months later, before my graduation, and as I began to accept the fact that I was an soon-to-be-unemployed student, I got an internship with Vs. Magazine (11) in New York City. It was a tiny but stunning fashion magazine that's "all around contradictions" according to what I saw one of the directors explain this to a makeup artist freelance during an image shoot.

When I received an email to schedule an interview, I couldn't recall applying to the company. I went to the website and on the top of it read"An Emotional and Curated Perspective of fashion and Culture.

OMG, SO EDGY! I was thinking.

Fashion Week rolled around in September. I'd been in the internship for nearly four months. There was no sign of a full-time job or an offer.

The fashion director and communications manager were able to get tickets to all shows during Fashion Week, but couldn't really attend all events, therefore they donated some of tickets to Interns (that's me!).

Hallelujah. We praise the heavens and earth. This is what I've been awaiting since when I attended the Chanel trunk show when I was just fifteen. I had the privilege of sitting on the second and first rows throughout the entire week, it was a dream coming real.

I was able to meet an editor at the top of the chain of Lucky Magazine (12) I have met at a previous fashion show that was exclusively for press and was the Resort Collections of a variety of designers. The collections take place between the The seasons of Fall/Winter and Spring/Summer, and are held a few months prior to Fashion Week. The collections are designed for individuals who enjoy holidays in the tropical heat of winter. Not kidding.

In the end, I attended the press conferences to meet the creator, Zimmermann (13). I was a huge fan. I'd had conversations with the Lucky Editor, but I only learned her initial name.

The next two months trying to find out her identity. Instagram, nope. LinkedIn, nope. Just before Fashion Week, Lucky Magazine included her in one of the posts they posted on Instagram. It was at least the Instagram tag. It wasn't until a few days later that I realized that I should have checked out that masthead on the magazine, and the credits page. What a fool.

I didn't have any way to get in touch with her (this was prior to Instagram Direct) till I met her, once more at Zimmermann in the Fashion Week show for Spring/Summer 2014. (The shows are held one year prior to the time that collections hit the streets and this was in the year of the summer 2013 and which was the year during my time at the internship.)

I saw her in the middle of the row, right in my face, talking with her colleagues, and appearing elegantly chic.

Oh my god, what a slobbering twit.

All was going well. I was not offered a position in Vs. Magazine because they did not have any new full-time employees but that was okay because I had just decided that I would get an opportunity at Lucky the magazine, which was which was a Conde Nast publication. I was on the road to becoming a fashion editor in real life.

I was totally outside my comfort zone.

I was not paying much attention to the show. I was too busy imagining the conversation I was having in my mind. I would say "Hey, remember me?" all casual-and-totally-not-terrified, and she would say, "Hey, of course I do!" Then she would tell me about an opening at Lucky for a junior editor and that I was just perfect for it because she could already tell I was chic and perfectly Lucky. (See the way I phrased it?)

The show came to an end and I only had a couple of moments to find her prior to the audience ran to towards the exit, and I ended up losing her. When I wrote the story written in my head. My expectations and the reality would match perfectly, after all, isn't that the way it is?

I was frozen.

In my grave.

I would never be able to talk to her! She contacted me during the press conference since she didn't realize that my role as an intern. If I were to give her my resume and be accepted for a job, I could not keep this lying any longer. I'd need to admit, in the open that I was an intern in a low position. She couldn't believe me. She was awe-inspiring and was sitting at the top of the row of the biggest runway show. Only extremely successful and totally untouchable individuals can achieve this. I am not brave to imagine she'd be able to talk to someone similar to me?

People who are on the first row typically are photographed by paparazzi swarms. Photographers may not be aware of what they're looking for, yet they think that because they're in the front row, they're significant. Sometimes they're right , but sometimes they're completely wrong.

Model-off-duty Amazons were being photographed on the runway. They, also, appeared to be a bit intimidating to be a conversation with.

Then I saw a small girl who appeared to be around six years old with a better outfit than I'll ever get, approach any of them being photographed by at the least 12 paparazzi. The little girl. She was likely the daughter of the woman.

Then, the moment when the light bulb went off.

The woman in question is a mom. She's changed diapers for hundreds of children. She's likely been peed on. She's probably not all so frightening. She's no different than The Lucky Editor right in front of me.

This Lucky Editor leaped and I waved my hand to get her interest. She instantly recognized me. She remembered we had been at the press event of the designer that was featured in the fashion show we had just seen and that she knew that I worked as an intern. How? It could be because I'm a foolish fool. However, she was a fan of me. Do you believe that? And neither did I.

After a few weeks, I was at Conde Nast to meet with her. Once security "granted the access" I walked up an elevator and into The Lucky office.

In fact, do not want to disappoint you, this security person actually told me, after only a few minutes of in the phone conversation about me "Miss Conway, you've been granted access."

It was a pleasure to visit the Lucky floor (other magazines that are within this building are Allure, Vogue, GQ, Glamour, among several other magazines) and had a chat with the Lucky Editor for over an hour about fashion, life and career plans. We discussed the type the job that I had been searching for.

Within a couple of weeks I received a call from her to inquire about an opening.

I didn't land the job at the final, but it's fine I'm over the whole thing. The job was offered to someone else, who likely was the son of a well-known editor or designer, which is the story I tell myself so I don't get sucked into sleep at night.

Imagine that The Lucky Editor was with her family brought her a sense of sense of humanity that she wasn't to be her "untouchable style editor in the front row" I believed she was. If I had let the crippling self-doubt or negative self-talk consume me, I wouldn't had been a candidate to be a part of Lucky magazine or have made an invaluable connection to people in the industry.

The daily struggle with negative self-talk, as weird family members, is something that everyone across the globe shares, however only a few have the necessary skills to beat it. Instead of dwelling on the things you're doing well and wrong , and all the ways that you can be a mess, think of the person who you're afraid of as an individual.

They're real. They have made mistakesand likely been pampered. Although we're all quite different, we're one in the same.

There's something incredibly soothing and positive about that do you think?

The importance of Authenticity

You are the person you are. That's the truth regardless of the place you go, you are. You can't avoid making changes or compromising your own. You could try to alter the way you look, just as every freshman does in their first year at college, but it's not lasting. You'll only be able pretend for a short time until you're back to being yourself.

It's fine simply being yourself. Actually, being yourself is amazing. Because you're awesome.

Being who you are will allow you to get through your life. It's the only way to meet and attract individuals who are living their lives in the authentic way.

First, you need to identify your authentic self, and then figure out what it means for you.

I was able to spend a lot of time wearing various costumes trying to figure this one out for myself. Take as long as you'd like exploring who you are. It is possible to be several authentic personalities through your entire life.

We're constantly changing, trying new things and adapting to our experiences, which bring fresh illumination to our personality.

I declared that fashion was my life's passion at fifteen. I spent the following years pretending that fashion was my obsession because, for a short time it was. However, I gradually grew tired of it.

As a teenager, I used to wear extravagant outfits on a daily basis. In college I grew more minimal. Now my uniform is jeans, a T-shirt, and chucks with the occasional feel-like-being-fancy day or night thrown in.

I began to see that fashion was not my thing at the moment. It had been for some time, but I wasn't able to fully comprehend that this was the case. Everyone I knew that I was the "fashion model." The one who was determined to break into one of the toughest sectors to enter, and was willing to do anything.

This part of me remains true. I've just discovered that I was following the wrong path.

When it is about "passion," we have some notions about it and what it's supposed appear like: that certain people have it, and others do not, and that it's the one thing that always gives us the energy we need and that you can have it all the time. It's too strong to be a temporary thing, as we think.

At the age of 15 I proclaimed this as my true passion, since at the age of fifteen I was a zealous teenager. I believed it was going to be for ever.

It wasn't until recently that I discovered that, as we change as individuals, we also change the things that motivate us and provide us with energy.

What I learned was that even though fashion isn't the case for me, it is my "passion," it does provide me with emotional satisfaction. I am awed by the imagination it demands, the craft as well as the historical context. I enjoyed my time during Fashion Week, the time I spent researching the industry, as well as the brief time I had to be a part of it.

While fashion is an integral part of my personality however, it's not the only thing I'm proud of or the most important thing.

When I figured this out, I was feeling like I'd lost something. The part of me that was a part of me was so important, what was I without my status as the "fashion woman?" Breaking up with this part of my identity was just like every other breakup and caused me to be devastated.

I quickly discovered that passion isn't a finite thing. It doesn't need to be a constant thing and you don't have to keep just one passion.

Being my authentic self doesn't include being "fashion girl," for now.

Don't be scared to live your most authentic life. It's okay to admit that it's not the things you once loved or that your love could now provide you with satisfaction in your life.

If you're not living your authentic self it's easy to attract people who align with your personality and not the real you. It's impossible to be able to meet wonderful people this way and establish genuine connections when you're portraying yourself as someone who you aren't.

Put your trust in yourself, in the heart of your, and do things that push you forward, and only with people who can help you improve.

If you don't feel like you're passionate about something you're not a bad person. There are probably a few that you aren't aware of. If you require a bit of help locating it, try these questions:

"I am unable to keep track of the time at times ..."

This will help you narrow the difference between what you consider to be satisfaction from your emotions and what's a passion. Write down three things. After that, write three more things. Next, you can go back and write another five items.

It's evident that once you're in the third and final round, it's a lot more difficult to come up with things, however, you'll see that you've got more skills and interests than you imagined and that many of them could be made into a business.

Takeaways

1. Making friends after college, or out of the office is really difficult.

2. It's important and come up with innovative methods to make new friends. You can go to bars by yourself. I'm serious.

3. A good word can be worth 1,000 openers. Be sure to never say, "What do you do?"

4. Do not engage in conversations with your friends. Open and vulnerable as soon as you can.

5. Going out on your own is a rewarding experience however, if you'd like to be more specific such as knowing the types of people will be in the area you should look

at meetup.com as well as Eventbrite in order to locate groups that are more specifically suited to your interests.

6. I would not recommend to sleep on the floor of Central Park and running through the Bethesda Fountain. However, it's all can be a good story, right? The people I've met and the experience I experienced.

7. Be mindful of your choices. Be accountable for them. Live in them.

8. The worst thing that could happen by doing this kind of thing can be... absolutely nothing.

9. Make friends with your family. They're yours and it requires less energy than being angry at them.

10. Imagine powerful individuals with their families. I'm betting that their families are genuinely strange. Then, it's an easy thing to get them to talk to you. Because even gorgeous models can puked on.

11. You are who you are. Unapologetically. Always.

Chapter 4: Building the Courage

INTROVERSION VI. EXTRAVERSION GETS much attention recently (14). It's now clear that neither is superior to the other in addition to the a lot of advantages for both. I get my energy back when I am alone, however, after I've refueled, I require a way to release all that energy to spend time with other people. As such, while I lean towards an introvert, I also have inclinations towards both.

My introversion may hinder my encountering new people. I get caught up within thinking about the "what-if's" about it and only think about the negative side of things. What happens if people don't like me? What happens if I'm turned down? What if I don't connect with any one and look like an idiot for being on my own? The two most significant aspects of introversion that I've had to realize was one, was the need to be alone and the habit of living completely within our heads. you're always thinking and when we're thinking it's just an issue of time before it turns negative. However, extroverts aren't in any way immune to this. Both sub-identities have a lot of overlap.

A lot of extroverts recharge their energy through social interaction However, being a solo person isn't the easiest thing for those who are more introverted. Going out on your own means that you've left your defenses behind. You're not protected by the protection of your team This is precisely why it's extremely efficient. The strategies I discuss within this section were developed by an introvert. However, they're applicable to everyone. They function as psychological nudges. They are things you could use in the crowd when you're trying to get to know people, meeting a brand new person, or even lying in bed trying to force yourself to get out of the room.

The first thing to do is read knowing that you'll make changes in your life that people think about only in their head.

Disclaimer: Things are going to get strange.

In addition to my previous suggestion of visualizing powerful people and their families, here are seven nudges that I've employed to make me want to meet wonderful people. The process began without nudges or at the very least, conscious ones. However, I began to pay attention to the factors that prompted me to leave the cozy embrace of my comfortable zone. Here are my tips.

1. Do the hard thing

My first home in NYC was located on one of the Upper East Side of Manhattan that was famously portrayed through billionaires as well as Gossip Girl. I was a few blocks away from that Gossip Girl stomping grounds in the one bedroom apartment which was converted into a two-bedroom unit with a wall made of artificial. It was simply it was a complete sh*thole.

Even though it was in a safe area however, the apartment was in complete disarray.

I experienced gas leaks that the landlord didn't really fix despite his assurances and cockroaches, mice, and a traumatic break-in.

It occurred just one week prior to Thanksgiving 2014. I was not sleeping well and was shifting and tossing around for the majority nights. The weekend was filled with friends and cousins who had visited and a stomach overloaded with unhealthy food and drink caused me to be awake for a long time.

I awoke for the third or fourth time in the night to see someone waiting in the doorway of my bedroom. He was wearing an unisex white T-shirt with a V-neck along with brown glasses and a beard. The baldness of his head sparkled in the dark.

He wasn't aware the fact that I'd observed the man, and I shut my eyes and was dead. This was, according to me that was my best chance at survival. So long as I didn't believe he was seeing his face, I was safe.

I went on for three to four hours lying down and figuring out combat and flight strategies. What could I make use of to make a weapon in case I required to fight?

What would be my ideal strategy of escape in case I were to escape?

My mind wandered to places it's previously not explored. I allowed myself to contemplate about how I could kill this man if I had to, and had the opportunity or, even more worrying, about what might occur to me if were unable to escape or fight to defend myself.

The reality began to set in and I was in the survival instinct. The truth is that I was five feet four, 115lbs. and had nearly no strength in my upper body. If this guy would like to overwhelm and hurt myself, then he certainly could do it and there was no way to stop it.

However, survival mode is a powerful force and speaks louder than the reality that you have to stand up for yourself and not quit. Your life depends on it.

I woke up at 7:45 am. I snoozed my alarm and surveyed the room. He was gone just as quietly as he had been when he had.

He never touched me. My computer sat right on my bed, and my jewelry was on hanging display that I had on the wall.

The thing which scared me the most was the realization that he wasn't in the area to take anything. He was not even in my presence to harm me. The man was just there to supervise me.

Over the next couple of days, I felt obsessed with the fear. I experienced nightmares that were violent and entailed some sort of threat scenario.

It was everything I'd thought of happening that night, but they never came to pass.

I didn't know why he didn't harm me, or why the man sat there on my sofa on the wall next to my bed, watching me while I tried to fall asleep. I was obsessed with thinking of scenarios where he might come back, however, the next time, it was to do something different than his bizarre idea of entertainment. Nightly panic attacks were a regular routine that continued for the following months after the night. Like everything else once a certain amount of time had was up and the anxiety attacks and nightmares.

I later found out that the man who was sitting over me , was actually the locksmith employed to work for the company.

I decided to get out of the apartment. I could have purchased a security camera as well as changed the lock but due to the man's skill and his knowledge, it was not a matter of what number times I switched the locks. I moved back home to stay in my parent's home for a while I also traveled during the month following that, and moved in the NYU building in the entire summer of 2015, the following day, September 1, 2015, I signed a lease for a second time in the Bushwick neighborhood of Brooklyn.

I could have allowed myself to be trapped in that fear for a lifetime. I might have been scared of leaving and move back into New York, and to take a step forward in my life.

I could have allowed the fear of a attack consume me.

Instead, I allowed myself to be numb for a few minutes. I let the sleep-related panic attacks to take place with the knowledge that they won't be a constant thing.

I'd heard a lot of people saythat "pain is never permanent" and I decided that it was true. them.

The transition to NYU was a challenge for me, as I had no idea what to expect and almost no money, however, I knew that I had to take action, something to help me get back on the right track.

The simplest option was to let fear rule the day.

The most difficult thing was learning to grow and be more of a person.

Do the difficult thing.

Making the Hard Choices in your Everyday Life

As my alarm clock goes off each day, I tend to lay on my bed and think, "I could totally sleep in today.. That's right, I don't have a lot to do. I could go to sleep for another hour." As freelance, my work schedule is totally my own and that's great. But until it's not. It's a negative thing in the event that my embarrassing habit towards lazyness seeks to play devil vs. angels with me.

However, laying there for the whole day is the easiest thing to do and I'm aware that even though it feels like it's going to be fantastic sleep isn't going to be beneficial in the longer term. The majority of the time the easiest thing to do isn't the one that's worth it. Therefore, I ask me, "What's the hard thing?"

As much as I don't like it, the hardest aspect is always getting up and do things that I know my future self would be grateful to me for. Sometimes, the things I must complete during the day aren't likely bring me instant gratification However, I'm sure they'll be helpful to me further down the line. It's not something we do however it's the most difficult task to complete. It's also worth the effort. Do the difficult thing.

The easiest thing to do is to sleep in and turn on Netflix and go through three (actually 10) minutes of One Tree Hill and put off doing things that won't provide me with immediate satisfaction.

However, badasses do not take the easy way out. The first step is to make making a commitment to yourself.

Make yourself promise to be able to make the difficult task worth it, and that you won't be waking up in the morning to no avail. Do your best and be smart. Make the lifestyle you wish to liveand then move forward each day.

If you are confident that you'll make the difficult thing worthwhile, the difficult thing becomes an easy task. The strain of waking up each day is only temporary, in contrast to the agony of regret, loss of dreams and potential that isn't fully realized, doing the difficult thing is the preferred choice.

Attending this General Assembly conference that I've been talking about for a while was at the time the most difficult thing I had to accomplish. I'd just spent thousands of dollars and I didn't need to pay for an apartment. A dorm room? I've never done this since freshman year in college. I felt like an unqualified kid when I first moved in.

I purchased the ticket to the conference using my remaining 70 dollars. It was a long walk of for fifty miles through the New York City summer heat in order for food, I was unable to pay for a subway ticket and taxi. I attempted to instill a illusion of confidence by wearing a chic outfit, but I been sweating for hours when I arrived there. Due to the state I was at that time in my life and the circumstances that preceded the moment, arriving at Hudson Hotel Hudson Hotel on the first day of the conference all by myself, was one of the most difficult things I've ever had to accomplish.

Then the keynote speaker began to speak, and it was the easiest thing. I was exactly where I wanted to be. I was to meet my soon-to be business partner couple of minutes after. I would be greeted by the wisdom and words I required to listen to being surrounded by people who I soon discovered were "my my people."

The journey to the Hudson Hotel on the second day of the conference by myself, was the most easy thing I've ever been required to do. These fifty blocks along with the sweat that arose from them, gave me proud instead of ashamed. It seemed like the walk would pass through in just a few minutes.

Due to my promise to myself and those moments of intense feeling of discomfort, which transformed into a sense belonging, the difficult task became easy. I made a commitment to myself that I would make decisions that were going assist me over the long run and not just in the short-term.

Do the difficult thing, as you might surprise yourself and transform it into something easy.

2. Recognize the two types of fear Part 1.

There are two kinds of anxiety. These are those that stop people from being in life-threatening situations, such as not being able to walk alone through dark alleyways, or doing nothing when a shady person is in your bedroom. There are other kinds of fears that have no use or any purpose, such as the fear of being rejected.

This section will focus on the type of fear that first comes to mind.

After the burglary I was plagued by a variety of different nightmares. Most of them involved some sort of violence. These were the scenarios I considered as I lay in bed in bed pretending to fall asleep.

They came about as a result of my unconscious seeking a outlet for the fear that had accumulated within me while I listened to the person breathing deeply while he watched me.

In one vision I woke up in a warehouse that was abandoned with an armchair in the middle of the empty space playing with a gun that was within my left hand. I was wearing a kind of cargo pant that let me to put a tiny handgun inside the pocket.

I moved my way around on the chairs that appeared to have been abandoned from what could be an old office.

I did not have confidence in the way I used my gun. I was playing as it was a toy. Mystic, I fiddled with the gun in my pocket, and accidentally shot myselfby firing the trigger and hitting my left hip. It didn't kill me. From an outside-of-body viewpoint I watched myself bleed out until I woke. In those months of panic attacks and nightmares I thought about the idea of purchasing guns. While I'm not able to say whether it was true, I believe my subconscious was telling me not to buy one because it would eventually cause more harm.

This dream happened only one time, as did many other dreams however, it was one that kept frequent.

I would awake, even though I was still in the dream and would see a gigantic dominating me.

Every at night, those that chased me were diverse. They were threatening and appeared to have the sole purpose of scaring me.

I would look at them, still in my dream, but I would think I was awake and would revert back to survival mode , just like I did in the past when the same situation was happening.

Heart racing, sweaty palms and paralyzed by the fear of what could have happened.

They looked so real. the only thing that made them appear unreal was their height. They always had a massive build and an ogre-like body. Their faces were distorted like they were made out of stone. In essence, they all looked like the Hulk but certainly not way that resembles Mark Ruffalo, brooding and emotionally damaged manner. (15)

The vast majority of the monsters I imagined were terrifying but there was one exception.

The only one who was not scary was the one who wore an ear-to-ear smile while he sat in the wicker chair that was in my bedroom, snatching at the chunks of wooden.

He would rise to play with the same enthusiasm as a puppy that was not trained. And, exactly like a puppy the room was filled with him seeking attention and a friend for him to have fun with.

I soon became quite attracted to him, so I gave him the name. Freaky Freddy. He was a lot as Roald Dahl's Big Friendly Giant.

I decided that he needed some background information. I wanted to ensure that the other terrorists would never come back The best method I could think of to accomplish this is to create them into the most real-life version I could and take them from my subconscious to my conscious and then take the power away from them. This involved the bringing of my terrorists to the light of day.

In acknowledging him and making him more real I was able to defeat both him as well as his frightening comrades and eventually.

I thought Freddy was a little boy however, he didn't appear like the other gigantics.

He didn't fit in much. In giant society I thought, they were believed to be a threat to humans, yet no one was aware of the reason. Humans were simply not used to giants, which meant they were an enemy. To counteract this threat they tried to scare us away from them, so that they wouldn't be afraid of us.

The characters of Monsters, Inc. learn that harnessing the human laughter provides cities with more useful energies than harnessing the human voice thus they overcome their fear of human race. I wanted to demonstrate to Freddy how to impart the same lesson to other giants.

Freddy did not like the idea of scaring people. He loved human race. He loved the world wanting to be part of it. However, he was never accepted due to his size. Humans would always be afraid of him, despite the best effort he made to show that he was safe.

Being bullied in the high school setting, I can understand his struggle.

I felt bad for Freddy. It was my desire to become his buddy and show him that human beings were not scary, and that he was in the right place to want to know us better.

Freddy was determined to teach other giants to be nice to humans , but he didn't know how to begin. The man who was his father, the one with the greatest frightening of the giants and their chief. Everyone in the village was awed by him.

Freddy was a disappointment to his father as Freddy was not a fan of scaring people. He always tried to make friends with us and his dad was not happy with him.

However, his father was afraid of getting to get to know us. As Freddy who was unaccustomed to us Humans were not familiar with the giants.

However, we can stop being scared of one another by learning from one another. We could live in our communities without fear or war one another.

I wanted to assist Freddy show the other giants that they don't need to be scared by myself or anybody else.

Before I could help him, he disappeared.

Freddy isn't aware of this I'd like to could have told that to him. But he has changed my life.

I'm sure that he's not real however, in my dreams it felt like he was real. The presence of Freddy in my bedroom was just as real as the real person who triggered my subconscious to create him.

He would be in my desk chair and smile with the joy that only children can have.

It was likely that he was instructed to follow me, and that I'd be an easy scare just like the other big beasts. However, Freddy did not want to make me feel scared. He was aware of the reason that he was there but he couldn't get away without it.

I conquered my fear of gigantic creatures by making them actual. In lieu of being able to avoid them and pretend that they didn't have the space in my mind I allowed them to live there. I let them live in the space they desired. However, they wouldn't have rent-free access.

My defense stopped or showing them my fear, and they went towards frightening others.

Maybe Freddy found the courage to prove to them that they don't have to worry anymore. humans aren't as scary because they don't view us as if we're scary, the way we look at the giants.

I was aware that not addressing my worries could only make them stronger.

I discovered that turning them into something funny like a cartoon by naming them as real, and giving them relatable backstories will take away their power and help them grow.

I wouldn't've had any chance against the giants weren't because of Freddy. Freddy was there to help me gain the courage necessary to hold tall against the other.

When I would look at the huge, terrifying ones, I felt overwhelmed. I was scared by my mind's efforts to keep it in check which would've been simple to allow it.

To be successful, I had to regain control. Our minds are powerful , and even though it might seem as though we're not in control, in reality we have everything is needed. Instead of not addressing your fears and turning off from them take a step back and acknowledge your fears and accept them. The fear is similar to a bad lover Once the chase has ended, so too is the chase.

2. Recognize the two types of fears Part 2.

The second type of fear that isn't there to protect us from harm and can only harm us in the end is the anxiety of being rejected.

Both kinds of fear stem from evolution, however this one needs to be learned.

Do not let fear prevent the action you want to take, make use of it to help you understand what you ought to be doing.

I began to see patterns in the things I was scared of. My anxiety was rooted in the choices I made, my capacity to succeed or the negative consequences of not succeeding. What happens if nobody likes me? What if they do? It's only an issue of time until they realize my weaknesses.

I realized that, regardless of the source the more frightened the idea made me feel, the more beneficial it could be. I had to be confronted with this fear a number of times and then overcome it many times in order to recognize the patterns. It never became easy to overcome until I came to understand its strength, I realized the fear-based emotion for what it truly was. If it weren't so painful breaking a bone you'd continue to live with the injury, causing the body parts to become unusable. Fear is the emotion that signals you're on to something. There's something in this moment that you need be aware of. Something is happening right at the moment, and your mind would like to know about.

The fear of rejection is a frightening thing and can numb people into confusion. If you sense your fear rising take the time to acknowledge it instead of becoming overwhelmed by it.

We can all agree that rejection isn't fun, however it's usually not fatal to us when we're alone in dark alleyways could be fatal.

Fear of rejection can hinder you from trying something new and making new friends.

Our gut instincts are telling us that major changes are approaching; that what's going on is not clear and human nature is designed to stay clear of uncertainties.

It's simple for our imaginations to imagine negative scenarios about being rejected.

The reason our brains do this is as a way of avoiding suffering. This is fine, it's instinctive however it's not good for us. It's not a way to keep us alive with regard to evolutionary progress.

Only harm that it does to us is perhaps a temporary affront to our self-esteem.

Be aware of your instincts and let your anxiety build up when you're ready to go crazy, and then you do it.

The willingness to fail with accepting the fears as part in the learning process and perhaps being able to make it a productive aspect of it, is the place where your wonderful new friends are. The more scared you are more so. Your brain can trick you into following your fear, but not through dark streets or in the mouth of Tigers.

3. Act as if (16)

There are many images of people we'd like to be like. If you've never dreamed of becoming besties to Jennifer Lawrence, then you and I share fundamental differences that we'll probably never overcome.

There's a certain kind of person that we all wish to be. I would like to be hilarious similar to Amy Schumer and Melissa McCarthy and talented as Jennifer Lawrence and Lupita Nyong'o and effortless as Julianne Moore and dazzling as Emma Watson.

I'd also like to be Paul Rudd's spouse. The problem is that this job is not available.

What if you were a mixture from Amy Schumer, Melissa McCarthy, Jennifer Lawrence, Lupita Nyong'o Julianne Moore Emma Watson, and Paul Rudd's wife?

What would the person do?

Do they want to sit back to watch life change around their heads? Would they be able to integrate themselves in the way they wanted to live? Do they build the community and life they wanted?

Of course, they'd choose to do the second. Because the mix of all these people could be awesome.

What is the outcome if you don't appear as you do? What would happen if you behaved as if you were mixture with Amy Schumer, Melissa McCarthy, Jennifer

Lawrence, Lupita Nyong'o Julianne Moore Emma Watson, and Paul Rudd's wife?

Wouldn't you love to be awesome?

Uh, yeah.

If you behaved as you were this person you could accomplish anything you want. You could rule the world without having to ask any questions or even thinking that's not really what you were supposed to do.

If you make it appear as if you're someone else, or the "kind that person" who is doing something that you're not used to and you fool your brain into allowing you to perform things you'd like to do but believed that you could not.

You're just acting, at the end of the day.

It is important to understand that acting like an individual is not an effective method to lead your life each day. Being yourself is the only way to live a life that's sustainable. This is to fool your self into doing what that you aren't sure you're capable of doing, the things that your introverted side would like to prevent you from doing.

You might have difficulty expressing yourself at social gatherings. What would someone who's the main attraction at a party do? They'd meet new people. They'd be confident and social.

What could happen if you behaved like an ebullient social butterfly?

You could be fooled to appear comfortable social butterfly.

It's all possible if allow it to be. You can be anyone you'd like to be. All you need to do is pretend to be. Make it appear as if you're loved one of all your heroes and turn out to be just as amazing as that person should they ever exist.

We're trying to be around people who are a bit of a badass since it's likely to cause us to become badasses as well. Challenge yourself to your limits and pretend to appear to be that "kind that person" who shows up at a party by themselves and join a hiking group without a companion doing the same, and speak to strangers in hopes to become their friends.

You'll be amazed. Because you're unlimited.

If we're not consistently getting better, we're not doing anything meaningful. Our flaws lead us to believing that we aren't able to or should not do something that could actually be quite simple to accomplish if we change our perspective to look at our own self-perception differently.

If it's not that easy then, just do the difficult thing.

4. Let Your Ego Win

I just had to go to a bar on my own one time for people to consider it to be impressive. Many people believe that they aren't capable of doing anything similar to that, and the first reaction is to be awed when they see another person doing something similar.

Then I allowed myself to feel great about myself and feel happy about myself. Therefore, I keep returning to see what else I can do.

I'd like to feel the same good feeling over and over and over and over repeatedly. I love knowing that someone is amazed by me. I love being satisfied for having done what most people don't do but not because they couldn't however, but due to fear.

When I first told someone that I had gone out on my own and made cool new acquaintances, and had planned to meet them for the next time, I was greeted with a shot of serotonin, and an approval. It was a drug giving me the high I knew I needed to experience again.

I was hooked.

I felt the happiness be felt as they said "I would never be able to do this." "Yes you can," I wanted to declare. "You simply have to choose for not."

I would continue encouraging people to be amazed by me for doing the things that they would never to do. First time that I walked by myself was a challenge. I had to face the fear of being rejected and feel uncomfortable in a environment until I could summon enough confidence to talk to someone.

However, the next time around was not nearly as challenging because I had a motivational factor. There was also the benefit of knowing that I was likely be slapped with a second dose of serotonin, and also acceptance.

I was a normal addict.

Even if I didn't make cool new acquaintances I had a funny or embarrassing story to tell.

As I did when I met two bankers who were investing and pretending that I didn't know anything concerning New York. I thought it was amusing for me to get "taken off" instead of having to think of ideas.

However, if we're real, I was just looking to entertain myself. They appeared like some goons. I was sure, at best, I would have a laugh from the night.

I didn't think it was a mistake to believe they were scumbags.

The two bars they took me to were among the most sexiest bars in Manhattan. In retrospect, the evening, it's likely they were interns. It was the time of year for interns, and internship season now underway. They claimed to be twenty-five years old, but looking back I could have concluded that they were most likely just turning 21.

The first clue should have been the time they asked me if I would like to shoot Fireball shots.

Yes, I do not want to shoot Fireball shots. Swipe left.

Most people will advise that in order to succeed, you need to be able to shut down your self-esteem at the door. Most of the time, this is the case.

We're all humans and all of us want acceptance from fellow humans and even strangers. Everyone wants to feel happy, look good, be attractive to others and have something unique to give that other people don't.

If you've done something difficult to perform, something that people tend to always avoid throughout their entire life, such as going out with a friend, be sure to tell everyone you can. Make use of the reactions of others as a reason to continue doing it and feel great about it.

The further outside of your comfort zone the greater the reward.

I went through a time in college that involved constantly cutting my hair. I had it up to my shoulders, and then cut it so that it was just below my shoulders, and then down to my chin. Then I cut it off and became a pixie several years ahead of Jennifer Lawrence and Anne Hathaway were able to do it.

The first cut I made was totally liberating. It was like becoming a new person. I was hooked on the sensation and the reactions I experienced when I did something that most women wouldn't cut off their hair.

Give your self-esteem a boost and become an awe-inspiring person. If you're out by yourself and you have difficulty communicating with people all you have to imagine them as their families. You're probably poopy.

5. Don't forget the Benefits

Delayed gratification is a component of the equation and I'm sure you'll get it worth the wait. Sometimes, when other nudges don't work for me, I'll use this as the icing on the cake. It's guaranteed to make me get up in the morning and off of Netflix each time.

It's easy which is what makes it so wonderful.

Keep in mind the advantages.

Remember the wonderful opportunities that can be created when you let them happen, when you take a step out of bed and push yourself beyond your limits, and place yourself into situations in which you meet new people is a possibility.

There aren't any benefits other than lethargy which result from watching Netflix throughout the day.

However, there are certain advantages to traveling the world and meeting new people, getting educated in the field you are interested in and then becoming the sexy person you've always wanted to be.

Do it. Take a step out of bed. The benefits are endless and so are your benefits.

While I was in San Francisco working an event for the company that provides management consulting I was employed by, I made the decision to travel a couple of days earlier to allow time to take in the city. It was my first visit to San Francisco and I wanted to set aside some time for explore. I managed to transport myself from my hotel close to the airport which is where the event will be held and then up to Pier 39. I was able to get through in the underground by asking every person I met whether I was going towards the proper direction and also the most appropriate stop to leave. Being lost in a unfamiliar city, however daunting it can be most enjoyable experiences I've experienced.

When I'm out walking on a gorgeous August afternoon in the city, taking in the sights and savoring one of my ice cream cones I see a vendor that offers boat tours to view Alcatraz along with The Golden Gate Bridge from the water. The very low cost (for the tourist attraction) provided two glasses of beer as well as two bottles of wine along with the tour. It's a no-brainer. It was definitely an attraction for tourists. However, I was a tourist. A thirsty one.

I ate my ice cream cone and strolled around along the pier until it was time to get aboard. The majority of other passengers were foreigners and couples and I soon became friends with my first passenger, a elegant late twenty-something from Tennessee. The hipster San Francisco had gotten to him. His man-bun was an obvious sign. I had 2 PBRs and I, being the slender woman I am, offered my number at the conclusion of this Instagram-worthy journey.

Was I thinking? I didn't. Could he've killed me and then raped my body? Yes, he could. However, it didn't happen. Instead he took me to a few hidden locations in the city, and to a tapas restaurant in the city after a short hike.

The advantages were obvious The message was clear: trust him and be shown San Francisco, and have an unforgettable day.

Living in fear of what-could-happen-but-probably-won't keeps you from trusting people who just want to take you to get tapas. Be aware of the benefits. It's always worth it to take the risk.

The Simplest, Last and most Important Nudge

This is the most effective one. It's the most simple and most crucial. It's also one of the hardest to master.

I'd like to share with you something you might not be aware of because the majority of twenty-somethings don't have this information. It's possible to say it all we like, but relying on that's the way to go is the only way to get it.

You're doing great.

I'm serious. You're fine. Do not worry.

It's essential to consider the choices we make when we enter our 20s because that's the moment we decide who we're going be, but we won't ever stop making these types of decisions. We never stop changing.

We must strive to create the life we envision to live in the coming years However, your mistakes won't stay for ever. Be assured that life isn't always going to go according to plan in this moment.

Comparing yourself with other people or being jealous of a individual's achievements or putting yourself down and dwelling on self-pity won't get you anywhere. I promise.

Furthermore, you're a lot of a badass to be lost in all of this. You're certainly cool enough to not stay in the mindset of scarcity and be apathetic when others achieve success.

The scarcity mindset is based on the assumption that there's a limited amount of success for the world, and if you're competing with someone else, it won't be enough to spare for you. Likewise, an the abundance mindset is based on the belief that the fact that someone else is enjoying the success does not mean that you shouldn't. This way of thinking instead of sabotaging the accomplishments of others or being disapproving, you celebrate their success and feel truly happy with them. (17)

There's a crucial thing I'm going to talk about that is privilege. Our challenges are real, sure, but they do not include getting the right water source for your family to survive, getting away from terrorist groups, or receiving a basic education. Growing in suburbs of New Jersey, being provided with an education in liberal arts with parents who are supportive of every one of my crazy ideas, I'm content with the life I've been blessed with. It is never easy to work hard however, I am confident that I'll never be truly being hungry, which is a relief that many people aren't able to access.

The subway ride through New York City is never boring. There's always something to look at. On one particular occasion, during the daily-rejection-from-the-fashion-industry period of my life, I was riding the subway and a homeless man who looked to be about my age boarded. I was experiencing a horrible day. I'd recently received a second rejection from a position I really wanted and would be really successful at, but was not paying attention to any other person. It's difficult to determine who is lying and which ones are scamming you. However, I could see it the look of genuine concern in his eyes that he was not scamming anyone. He started as most homeless people on trains do "Excuse me, everybody I'm sorry to interrupt. I wouldn't have to do this if I wasn't forced to."

I turned my attention to him, eager to listen to the story. He was just graduating with a degree in Communication from Rutgers. His parents had passed away in a crash one year prior and didn't have a lot to leave. He was left without money or parents and no work, no place to go and had no hope to change his situation. I wanted to offer him everything I could but I had no money in my pocket. Why would I believe I've been in a struggle? It could be me. My parents may die today I could be unemployed, homeless and penniless and have no way to make any change.

I got off the subway four stops prior to when the time I had to leave. I was laying at the foot of the sidewalk and cried at a rapid pace, not paying attention to about anyone who noticed me. I was suddenly faced with the universal truth that is oft-forgotten the importance of circumstances. Everyday rejection and failure was very exhausting, difficult and arduous, yet I was still able to have my parents. More importantly my father is an expert in financial planning. I'm sure that he is to deal with the unexpected. There will be no need for me to sleep. I'll never be hungry. I will never ask people for money in the subway. My privilege is huge. Although I was always aware of this the moment that I experienced it has made me more aware. The challenges I've had to face can be real. They have helped shape the person I am today. However, they don't include grieving over the loss of my parents, or trying to figure out my next meal.

The simple reality that you're reading this book, it means that you're connected to the Internet that means you've got a computer or at the very minimum, you weren't removed from the library as many homeless individuals do. Be grateful for your life and never stop helping others to live a similarly wonderful life, no matter what that might mean for the individual.

All we can do is to help other people and pass it on to others.

Always work hard. Build the life you would like to live so that you will live an amazing life, but above all , you want to ensure you can assist others to do the same.

Takeaways

1. Get yourself out of your familiar zone. You'll get to be able to meet some amazing people, boost your career, and assist you to become a total super-star.

2. Do the tough thing. If you do it, you might end up doing an easy task.

3. Make a commitment to yourself that you will always keep in mind the advantages.

4. Make fear the one that tells you there is a chance to achieve the heights of success. Let fear direct you to what you should be doing. But, you shouldn't be walking down dark streets in the dark.

5. Imagine that you're the you've always wanted to be.

6. Let others be impressed by your behavior when you are a bit sexy and use that as a motivation to continue playing

the game. Your ego could actually be to your advantage.

7. You're doing fine. You're a great person. Thank you and to help others.

Chapter 5: What to Do To be A Better friend

Great people attract great people. You are able to attend any number of meetings or conferences, events, and meetings as you wish However, in order to make significant connections with people who can provide immense worth to your business, you need provide a tremendous benefit to those around you.

In what I would like to refer to as "relationship utopia" this is the norm. However, the word "utopia" has many meanings that it is generally unattainable, and when it does happen it's a dystopian end result, as in each young adult book has taught us beginning with The Giver to The Hunger Games.

However, relationship utopia is possible and isn't a government overtake. It works the same way that we wish that our government would. Everyone takes part in making mistakes, and creating a positive atmosphere for all. There is no need to be flawless, but we need to always learn. We can learn by being aware of how our behavior can influence others, and then adjusting the way we behave to be positive instead of negative. The true utopia is in the effort we put into it. You're a wonderful friend to me, and I am a great partner to you within the bounds of human-ness.

Making concrete, actionable actions is what's needed to realize this dream. It requires hard work every each day. This chapter focuses on those practical steps, the aspects of our habits that have to be re-learned, the habits that we must break, and the new ones that will replace them, and finally, the attitudes that could alter our lives and our relationships and influence our outlook for the future.

"Accepting Bids"

Doctor. John Gottman, a psychologist and communication theorist is of the opinion that the secret to a successful relationship is in generosity and kindness (18). Well, duh.

But it's much more complex than the other. Small things are important, lots of them. Even the things that we're unaware of are important. In particular, those things we're not aware that we're doing matters in a big way.

Doctor. Gottman talks about the importance of "accepting offers" in every interaction. In essence, it's about accepting the possibility to connect, no matter how small or insignificant it might be.

Here's an excerpt of the article by Emily Esfahani Smith, published in The Atlantic, called "Masters of Love." I could not say it better So here's what Emily writes about it (19).

"Throughout all day long, spouses are likely to make requests for connections and that's what Gottman refers to as "bids." In this instance let's say your husband is a bird lover and sees a goldfinch flying across the backyard. He might tell his spouse "Look at this beautiful bird in the yard!" He's not just making a comment about the bird He's asking for a reaction from his wife, a indication of his support or interest. He hopes they'll be able to connect, even if only briefly or not at all, with the bird.

"The spouse now is faced with an option. She could respond by "turning towards" in the direction of "turning towards" to her partner or husband, as Gottman says. While the bird-bid could appear small and insignificant but it could reveal much about the quality in the marriage. The husband believed that the bird was significant enough to discuss it during conversation. The issue is whether she recognizes and appreciates.

"People who turned to their colleagues in the study engaged with the bidder and showing enthusiasm and support for the bid. The ones who didn't--those that did not reply or only respond in a minimal manner and keep going about their daily routines such as watching TV or reading the newspaper. Sometimes, they would react in a hostile manner with a statement like, "Stop interrupting me, I'm just reading."

"These bidding contests had profound impact on marital health. Couples who divorced after an interval of six years were able to "turn-toward bidding" 33 % of the times. Three out of ten of their requests for emotional bonding were accepted with a feeling of intimacy. Couples who remained in contact after six years of marriage had "turn-toward bids" at 87 percent of the times. In nine times of 10 times, they met the emotional needs of their spouse."

The scenario here concerns the husband and wife, but this does not exclude friendships that are platonic. In every interaction, you're faced with a decision. Whatever boring a goldfinch might appear to you the interaction that leads to "turning towards" as opposed to "turning against" creates connection and satisfaction for both parties.

"The 5 Languages of Love Languages(r)

The 5 Love Languages, written by a scientist Gary Chapman, examines the various ways that we display and receive love. Gary Chapman, the scientist responsible for writing this book about the subject (I refer to him as a literal wrote a book entitled The 5 Love Languages (20 21). Visit the page with resources) The book states there are five different types of love languages and they include:

Words of Affirmation

Acts of Service

Quality Time

Receiving presents

Physical Touch

Let's look at each one in detail.

Affirmations and Words

It is nice when someone you cherish says, "I love you," or "I'm proud of you" or "I am grateful for your." That's how you feel and respond to love and how you show it. You love hearing these words from people you love and you'd rather being unable to hear it for long. They can benefit from this information by telling them what you are trying to convey to them in every way feasible and you could perform the same.

Act of Service

You're all hot and irritable when someone makes a surprise for you. You might be working late, and someone you cherish stops by to offer you a fatty-ass sandwich from the deli you love or even runs the errands on your behalf when you're struggling. It's not their obligation to take care of these tasks for you however they will are willing to do it and you're more thankful.

Quality Time

The most important thing to you is spending time with the person you love whenever you can. It is your goal to spend the most quality time as you possibly can. It isn't a matter of what you're doing even if it's watching Netflix with a glass of wine, or taking off to a new adventure just you two. No matter what you're up to, it's important to do it with them.

Receiving presents

It doesn't need to be an Lamborghini or a Ferrari, but when someone you cherish comes to your house with a gift that surprises them even if it's your favorite candy bar you feel more connected to them. It's clear the thought that has been going through their head of your loved ones and that you've never appreciated even a tiny token. It doesn't need to be expensive or extravagant; simply knowing that someone has your thoughts on their list can make you feel happy and totally make your day.

Physical Touch

Physical contact can be expressed various ways. When it comes to romantic relationships, the physical may refer to sexual intimacy, when it's a platonic relationship, you can use usually a hug, or perhaps a high-five. Maybe this can answer your locker room buttslapping question?

Every person reacts differently to affection. If you are able to tap into the one your friend is most responsive to then you've hit the jackpot. There's a test that you can take to tell you which one you react with the greatest (22). You can find it on the resource page. I most often respond in response to Quality Time and Acts of Service.

It is crucial to keep in mind it is just because someone may be more prone to receiving Gifts rather than quality Time isn't a reason to assume they don't want to spend quality time with them once at a time. Spread these five love languages into your relationship.

Guys, this is completely free.

There is absolutely no cost. Zero dollars. The reward is huge.

High reward, low risk. This is what we like to see. If you're a good friend and show these kinds of affection whenever you can. People will be receptive and show the same to you. This seems fairly simple to me. Why do we not have this constantly? Because we didn't realize it. But now we know.

Sympathy against. Empathy

As we're discovering, there's actually a science behind having a better relationship with your friends.

We are familiar with the meanings of the two terms: Empathy and Sympathy. We are aware that sympathy refers to experiencing sorrow for another's unfortunate circumstances while empathy refers to the capacity to comprehend and feel our feelings.

There's a huge difference in how these two concepts are related to friendships, even but they're not that apparent.

Let me make one thing crystal clear prior to moving on that empathy is what you'd like to possess in every relationship you have ever had.

Being compassionate is more than just listening to someone else's struggles. It's about more than giving tips from an incident you've experienced during the previous time.

Empathy is the act of taking someone else's story and struggles, and imagine yourself as the protagonist. What would you feel when their story were about you? What would you do in similar situations? What's the most appropriate manner in which a friend will react to your story?

It's very easy to feel guilty for someone, but then distance yourself from their circumstances. We imagine, "That would never happen to me."

Empathy is the process of taking a circumstance and thinking, "But what if it happened?" When you shift your perspective such a way, you'll be able to see your entire relationship change as well.

People want to feel understood. They want to know that someone isn't going to say, "I'm sorry," but listen and connect in a more intimate way.

Sympathy says "At at ..." in the context of a friend's story of suffering. "At at least... the situation did not occur." "At most... it's not like you aren't suffering from cancer." "At at the very least... you know that your partner didn't cheat on your as Ashley did."

This reduces the significance of the struggle your friend is facing. It's like their situation isn't important, or doesn't seem to be the same as what's happening in your own life, or in the life of someone else.

Just because you or someone who you know is experiencing something challenging doesn't mean your friend isn'teither. The situation your friend is writing about isn't insignificant and when you look at your own situation with others you can lessen the hurt that your friend is feeling.

However, I can assure you that your friend will not feel her pain has diminished. The concept of sympathy is to maintain a superficial understanding of the circumstances. When you're empathic, as opposed to sympathetic and you believe that "that will never occur for me."

However, empathy involves imagining yourself as the protagonist of your friend's tale. What would you do? What do you feel? What would you do to get through it? In between the situation and not focusing on an underlying understanding of the issue, will totally alter your relationships to the good.

Watch the video, which is available on the resource page. which is voiced by Dr. Brene Brown (23, 24) who studies vulnerability as well as courage and shame. Check out the video to discern the distinction between empathy and sympathy.

The significance of self-discovery as well as Travel

According to another scientist Professor. Abraham Maslow (25) psychologist the 5 levels to human need. The theory is depicted as an inverse pyramid. It is impossible to satisfy the needs at highest level until you have filled those that are at the bottom of the pyramid.

The top of the pyramid serves our bodily needs, such as breathing, sleeping water, food.

Next is safety being secure in our environment. Then is love and belonging and esteem and finally self-actualization, more precisely, achieving all the potential that you can.

The possibility of achieving our full potential isn't something that humans consider until they are nourished and drinking water, shelter sexual emotions of security feelings of love and positive feelings about themselves.

When we have these needs fulfilled, we begin to consider self-actualization.

This is according of Maslow, the doctor. Maslow and, although I'm sure his wisdom and intelligence are top-notch person and all, I'll need to disagree from my own experiences. I've had self-actualization moments even when I'm not feeling at all self-confident, hadn't eaten for more than 24 hours, and even when I felt unsafe.

These moments always occur during my travels, and typically when I'm traveling on my own.

The experience of traveling with friends is similar to what's wrong with going at events, meet-ups and gatherings with friends who you don't speak to anyone else than the ones is already familiar to you. You tend to remain in your comfortable zone. This isn't your fault. You're just fulfilling the fundamental human need of being secure in your own environment.

We only seek out human connection with those that we're not comfortable with whenever we are forced to, and when we have no other choice, and when we're from our comfort zones that it's gone over the distance.

If I'm traveling on my own I'm (usually) lost I don't know the language I'm scared, alone, and I've nothing to do but seek assistance.

I need to find human connections and rely on the kindness and generosity of humans to come to get out of the mess I've found myself in. Since we both know that there's always something.

In my college years, I had the privilege of spending one period studying in Perugia, Italy (26). Although I am not trying to sound like another white girl who went to study abroad in Europe this was one of the most transformational experiences of my life up to the point at which I was. Then, the other memorable moments of transformation were also different travel experiences.

In December of 2011 the final month of my semester abroad I finally had the time to go to London for a visit with my friends doing their studies in London. I missed the train ride to the airport in the early morning (which could or might not be because I hadn't got back to my place the night prior to) I then I missed my flight.

I was unable to reach them due to several bad life choices which left me with an inoperable phone, twice. I was communicating with my friends on Facebook on the day prior regarding the specifics of my travel plans. I would be arriving at a particular airport, and then I would catch a specific train to a particular station, and then I would meet them at the exact location.

Since I missed my flight and was booked onto another four hours after I was forced to fly to a different location, at the wrong time, which meant I was in a train that was different to a different station. I finally made it to London in the middle to the center of London, then was able to get in line at the Information desk.

I tried to think of the questions I had in Italian prior to getting to the first line. I realized that I wasn't in a country that was Italian-speaking however, I was in one that spoke English! I believe I might have leapt up and down in exuberance, and not paying attention to the British observers.

It was an extremely long day.

The gentleman at the desk of information tried to assist me in the best way that he could, however, there was no money or euros, which meant I wasn't able to travel on the bus, and he only had a bus route.

He's certainly from the city's maps. He advised me on that I could use the bus however, that information was ineffective to me.

I went outside, glanced at the surrounding area, and then I saw the bus number 12. Wait, number 12. That's the bus that he said I should take! I chased it down and followed it's route the longest time I could. At least , I was heading toward the right way.

In the end, attempting to walk around for at most some miles, using only a map of the bus and no money to pay for the bus, I was able to find the street I knew by talking to my friends on the internet about where they lived.

Then all of a sudden I was able to physically meet my friend who I had planned to meet a few hours earlier at the opposite train station.

I was then able to being the subject of all jokes throughout the journey. My companions said they'd never been able walk from the station to their dorm and were astonished that I could navigate my way. It's true that I was pretty impressed by myself, as I'm not known for my direction-finding skills at all.

My London experience was more entertaining than it was exhausting unlike the time I arrived in Rome without any accommodation, and at the time that car bombs exploding on the streets were normal. By being vulnerable, asking assistance from the locals and relying on the kindness of people and compassion, I was able to secure a place to stay, without being attacked. Woo!

It's these moments that I'm hit in the face by self-actualization. "I achieved that," I think.

I have done it and that means I am able to accomplish anything.

If I am able to get back to home in a foreign land without any money, with no one near me however, with a difficult language, I will accomplish almost anything.

It's true that the "Let the ego take over" influence is present in this instance as well. Instead of letting others' positive feedback encourage me to do amazing things, it's actually how my feelings about me dealing with these situations on my own that gives me instances of self-actualization. This keeps me returning to do more.

I am constantly looking for situations that could be uncomfortable, awkward, and even a bit frightening to achieve my goal of self-actualization.

From these encounters, I've realized that the more opportunities for SA I experience and the more my junkie side is happy, the better friend I am becoming.

The more I understand the joy this experience can be The more I'd like to spread that shit around. The more I'd like to see my friends experience their own moment of SA and know that their full potential has been fully tapped into.

With this abundance and knowing that we will each have our own moments, I am more content as I spread this love wherever I go.

I'm looking for junkies to recruit, and you're the next.

The reason you should travel to locate Self-Actualization

I am blessed with the unimaginable pleasure to have grandparents that appreciate traveling above all other life-long learning experience. A classroom teaches facts; trauma teaches resolve; failure teaches grit; rejection teaches humility. Traveling teaches everything and more.

Nan and Pop are aware of this and insist that their children know this as well. In the beginning, Life is to Travel 101 included a trip for all eight of their grandchildren wherever they wanted to go around the globe to celebrate their 10th birthdays. I went to Paris and haven't stopped travelling since then every time I learn something new. I realized that I'm just dust in the breeze I am incredibly fortunate and, even though I understand why I'm not certain what makes the world go round , and kindness is their WD40 and most importantly, a willingness to be open to everyone and their diverse truths is the key to happiness.

I discovered this openness through every invitation I was given to immerse myself in the new culture. This involves going to people's homes to share dinner in their homes with families.

"You don't know them! How can you go into their homes that way! ?" is often the reaction I receive when I share these stories. Some people who have never experienced something similar to this would call it reckless, however those who have it's not the case. Never once did I feel risky or put in harm's way. In reality I felt at ease and comfortable.

I was always treated to an authentic, delicious homemade meal that was cooked at home and the chance to explore the language, as well as an insight into the importance of intercultural immersion.

Your mindset is one thing that is altered as you travel. It's not apparent at first however, it gets more pronounced and becomes difficult to control. I believe it's because traveling is a way of escaping reality, and that's why the decisions we make. You're more likely to think "oh heck, I'm in vacation! What's the problem?" "Yes" suddenly becomes the only word you're familiar with. When it happens, you will sense your serotonin levels increase just like if you're in love.

In those instances you discover that you're more real than in reality. In your work and at home you do the routine that you're expected do and the things you need to say "yes to, for instance, when your boss requests you to work on weekends as well as the things you must say no to, for instance, when a stranger invites for the meal with their family.

Relax and allow yourself to change your mindset. Travel. Find self-actualizing moments in thrill, the terror, and the swaying of reality.

If you can find it, you'll become an addict of a normal kind And you and I are bound to the same addiction.

The reason for this is evident the face of your opponent: "I don't have the funds for that."

The myth about traveling is that it is expensive and requires lots of money and that frequent travelers must be wealthy. It is possible to write a full book that proves that isn't the case and also the idea of travel hacking allows you to travel for a low cost and even no cost. However, this book isn't all about travel, so take a look at the resources page to find ways to master how to hack travel (27 28 and 29).

How being bullied in high School has shaped my adult Relations

"Slut!" she yelled from the hallway, when I was about go into the sophomore Chemistry. I looked around and saw her in the hall that was not occupied. We both left at the sound of the bell. She smiled at me with that smile she's become so adept in giving.

The one that caused my stomach to sink down to the knees.

A brief note: "slut" should be removed from our language as a species completely.

If she truly would have wanted to harm me, she ought to have said something that would be able to really hit me where it hurts. This was something I thought was real since I was sure there was no way I could be a womanizer in accordance with the definitions from the time I was a kid.

"You're slow at reading and everyone is convinced that you're dumb," or "You're a poor dancer, but no one would reveal it," would have hit far more closely to home.

Being a dancer of high quality was an integral part of who I was in high school. I always received attention because of my talent and if anyone had told me I was not good enough I would have been devastated. my confidence.

She obviously didn't finish her homework.

Yet, "slut" did the just the right amount of harm at the time she would like it to.

This wasn't the only or the last time she would attempt to intimidate me. High school was a four-year period that seemed like for a entire lifetime.

We used to be in the drama group together My bully and I. I knew that I was better at dancing that she, however my conviction in this knowledge faded over time. She sang, and that was the point where my talent ceased.

She was able to do both dance and sing, whereas I was able to only dance. She was able to play all the leading parts in the plays and it established a hierarchy among us, which was completely unintentional, but it affected our relationships regardless.

The lead lady and the girl in the chorus.

We were all in love with the same boy which is when things got a bit difficult.

"Lay it out. Tell her that you want to be her back. If she doesn't, Allison is your girl."

I read that through a text that was sent from my crush's friend's best friend towards my crush. The person who he "wanted to return" was me, my bully. The second one down, Allison, that one was me.

Heart: Shattered.

These 4 years in high school between 14 and 18, felt as the only ones to be concerned about. Teenagers are often viewed as if they're not real as if their issues aren't real issues.

Teenagers' issues may not revolve around the cost of a mortgage, or even saving for their children college tuition However, they're very real and frequently impact our lives and psychological well-being more than mortgage payment type of "adult" issues do.

These four years have made a profound influence on me personally.

I have learned a few things through this journey, perhaps the most important of which is that everyone has their own inner struggles and battles. Although they may appear to be in control but they're struggling with something we might not be conscious of.

We're all alike. Humans are, despite infinite variations, all exactly the same inside. Everyone is struggling. We're all trying to create our mark on the world. We're all worried about something.

My bully was bullied by me for liking the same guy she liked. She was aware that I was better at dancing then she. She was scared of me. The way she kept it hidden was to pretend to be more powerful than me, and actually hold me in her hands. Like I said earlier in chapter 1, she believed she was acting first.

In retrospect I could have spoke to her. I should have explained to her that she had hurt my feelings and the words she spoke could have a negative impact on me. I also told her that I was not going to be stealing her boyfriend. And I definitely wasn't planning to play her leading roles in the stage plays.

While I would love to try them but I never thought I would be able to be a singer of any quality.

I should have be nicer to her instead of being scared of her.

The lesson was that the old adage "love the neighbor you have" is true. you must be especially kind to those who aren't kind to you. They're the ones that require it the most.

I may have let this incident influence my judgement with concerns of trust. It could have been a way to let it hinder my ability to make new acquaintances, being vulnerable, and inviting people in. However, that would have meant she would have won.

She was not going to be victorious, but I was.

My four years in high school, but she wasn't able to have all of my existence. This is mine and only mine.

She helped me become more of a friend. Not only did I develop confidence and strength, but also a tough skin that has been useful many times in my life, she also taught me the strength to face her insanity, to learn from it, and improve my character as a result of it.

But despite it.

I'm more aware of people and our human nature is to "save faces." The woman wanted to avoid looking bad. Even though it was my expense, I am grateful to her for instructing me in a useful way. Be kind to everyone. Every person. Particularly, if they're unfriendly to you.

It was the Mount Everest of takeaways from this experience? No fucks for the people who hate you. There aren't many people who will love you, despite the best effort. Whatever their motives you are the only person in your life. Your achievements are yours. Your lessons are yours. Take them on. Enjoy them. Be nice to those who would like to take it off of you. Still, be nice to them.

Let's lighten the mood with A Story

I'd like to share with you about the most embarrassing chafing in my life.

To be clear It's not to be about getting rid of snarky friends or changing into more attractive. This is just a hilarious tale.

The most painful experience of chafing that I have ever had occurred when I was an intern at a clothing store during in the summer following my graduation from college.

It was the middle of a record-high heatwave that was sweeping through New York City. I was on the run with the newspaper I was employed by. I was required to deliver copies of the latest issue to the public relations reps of the designers we been highlighting in our editorials.

The editorials are the gorgeous photos at the rear of magazines. They're the arty ones and not the ads.

We would dress the models in designer clothes that they offered us for loan. Designers submit their latest designs to magazines in exchange for press for free.

The prestige of the publication depending on the prestige of the magazine, you could get stylish designers to offer you things for free in exchange for the right to showcase them.

The stylists have a variety of clothes they think would be appropriate for the editorial they're working on However, typically only a few pieces are selected for the photographs.

If they did not, we'd call the PR reps for the designers and inform them that we had featured the clothing of one of their clients.

We'd be willing to do this in the event that we want the designer to collaborate with us once more. They'll think, "Oh cool, I'm receiving press free from this magazine, and they've got interesting editorials. I'll even send them free shit." In the end that's what stylists would like, particularly for designers who had lower accessibility, such as Chanel, Valentino, Versace You know, all the big ones.

It takes time for stylists to establish relationships with the top fashion houses.

It was a pleasure to make deliveries in SoHo that is the priciest area in Manhattan. The prices are all high however the SoHo neighborhood is the most expensive. It's known for its architecture and shopping. But I'm not sure what the shops do to make their money.

Vs. Magazine The magazine I interned for has two issues a year. There's an issue for the Fall/Winter season and a Spring/Summer issue. To cover the whole period of six months, there's a lot of information that is incorporated into each issue and the result is quite large, and weighty, which is a good thing because it's so heavy.

"I have to get fit," I said several times throughout the summer, to my astonishment at having to carry multiple copies of this huge magazine across Manhattan.

I was scurrying around town throughout the day, handing out magazines to different representatives. I had just purchased new, lacy underwear that was adorable, but not what I was supposed to wear during this hot afternoon in

Manhattan as I carried about 50 pounds worth of magazines.

Rubbing and the rubbing, sweating as well, the sweating got worse. It was at first not too terrible. It was just the normal amount of chafing that you'd think of when wearing new clothes and underwear as your legs rub against each other during a scorching summer day.

Then it all happened at all at once. It went from not being at all bad, to being completely uncontrollable and I couldn't walk for a while.

It was my attempt to appear elegant, since it was SoHo and in extremely swanky offices for agencies to which I was applying for positions and was trying to conceal being an intern in the best way possible even though it is possible to observe one in NYC from distance of a mile.

They're carrying tons of crap and appear miserable.

I was unable to get up the stairs. "My legs are going to be bleeding," I thought to myself. "This could result in permanently scars."

My legs were massaged between two stick by the caveman who was desperate to make fire and have a hot food. Dry and raw I was in desperate need of relief.

After I had delivered my final package to one of the most sexiest offices and snappy PR representatives who didn't seem to care about me or the magazine I just handed over I took my underwear off and walked down the hallway.

There was a trash can located in the hallway. I immediately I threw them out. I didn't care who was watching. I briefly forgot my location. I was suffering too much.

I was so angry. That set of underwear was just so adorable. No one ever saw them.

In the end, I was being a commando wearing a short-sleeved dress. It was incredible.

I had to go back at the office of the magazine, and take a seat and fuck it. Maybe I should put a moist paper towel on my thighs and pray that nobody noticed.

As I went down the steps in The SoHo office building and felt like a completely different woman. How did I have no idea about this sooner? I could have avoided this completely. Or almost entirely.

Then, I rounded around to take the subway and return to my office.

And who was the person I ran into? A professor from a college. I don't have a clue what he was up to at the time in New York. I attended the college of Pennsylvania.

He could have told me that however what I was able to think of was my chafing, and the fact that I didn't even have underwear as I chatted casually with a professor from college.

Well, fuck. It's only New York.

Takeaways

1. Making friends with a greater understanding, and learning from this experience is all that counts.

2. The concept of relationship utopia is a real thing that exists in our efforts.

3. Take every chance to connect no matter how small.

4. It is possible to show affection in a variety of ways, as Gary Chapman wrote about in The Five Languages of Love Languages(r). Find out who you are with and which ones are yours and then sprinkle the all over the place.

5. Empathize rather than be sympathetic.

6. Travel.

7. Being able to recognize self-actualization moments makes you a better person and, consequently an even better friend. How do you find it? Travel.

8. Being being bullied in high school has taught me two things: 1. Be kind to everybody. People who aren't friendly to may need kindness more than you realize. 2. Don't be a hater.

Chapter 6: The Priority Game

"Nobody is ever too busy. It's a matter of priorities."

- Anonymous

Now , let's assume that you've already have a few tribe members. It's not difficult to talk to them , even if there's only one or two. What happens when your number increased or multiplied. Are you going to remove anyone you know they are valuable to you?

You don't. You control your time and your life according to this point . You must ensure that your tribe members don't feel as if they aren't needed any more. If they truly are part of your family, you should be able to spend time with them.

Many of the extremely busy people would be a bit surprised and then say they can barely manage to find time for themselves. This isn't the right approach to view some time off. The free time we have isn't just the gaps we find to fill in the gaps of our lives. The time you have free is not something you save when you make shortcuts or lists. It's the time we put aside to do something worthwhile apart from business and work.

When you receive an invitation nowadays, you look for your mobile or online calendar to see whether your calendar can accommodate the invitation. The problem is that you're not able to do anything do over the weekend, and then suddenly the following weekend is filled with activities you need to take part in. It's difficult to decide which one is the most important.

The majority of the time, it is better to pick important life events instead of things which can be put off. Events that are once in a lifetime are essential because they cannot be duplicated on the same way. Make sure to explain to other tribe members that you need to refuse the invitation for why you are selecting the life event over the invitation. If they're genuine tribe members, they'll recognize your decision.

Do not minimize the significance of the event you have chosen in order for the sake of making them feel happy. Why? Word of your thoughts can be spread to the other members of the tribe easily. If you declare that you don't wish to attend a relatives wedding, it could create a devastating rift between you and the person.

It's hard to make a decision and not having a choice is more difficult. Why? because you'd add two items to your list of regrets, instead of just one. If you opt to be neutral, no one gets to be able to see you and both invitations will be wasted. The feeling of affection and sentiment associated with that invitation will also disappear. The next time they invite people to attend a party or other life occasion it won't be your top priority since they'll remember that small gesture.

People who aren't able to keep their commitments are of the worst kind. If you are the one who made the promise, be sure to not be unclear. It can lead to many misunderstandings. If you're explicit, it may be a sting from rejection but at minimum, they're not wishing for anything. An absence of memories can be more painful than having both bad and good memories mixed up.

Do not say yes to every single thing. Don't double book invitations or events. Prioritizing events can make the your experience improve. There aren't lots of opportunities to meet people with busy schedules. You aren't the only one making changes.

Others in the tribe may have made the same mistake. Therefore, you shouldn't be able to just be a snob all the time because you tried your best to attend that gathering. It can be depressing when you focus on the possible consequences of your decision when you return to work or meet another friend you did not want to see. Accept the consequences of your decision.

Expect the same of the members of your circle. It will be more difficult once you reach the age of old together. Priorities change, so often the younger years seem so nostalgic since it was simpler to convince everyone to be on the same page and quicker. You shouldn't employ the same methods of scheduling you did when you were not married or had children. What you'd engage in would be different. It's difficult for members who are single in the tribe to get to know those who are married due to the fact that they have less in common , and the gap can be difficult to bridge in certain situations.

The spouses should be aware that their marriage must be in a balanced way. Singles should not necessarily be those who have to adjust. If the urban residents and suburban dwellers require a meeting, they should go somewhere in between. Find new places to visit, and discover gathering spots that allow them to bring their families along as well as have fun.

A compromise is the most effective solution for all issues. Don't be apathetic simply because it's difficult to schedule. Don't make someone who wasn't there feel guilty. This is not the purpose of getting together with friends. The goal is to make connections, with each other, not to be alienated. Technology today allows the inclusion of a person who isn't physically present.

This will allow the person to be part of the fun by explaining what you are doing at a particular moment. It's not easy to keep it going all the time. However, at a minimum the sensation of "wish you could have been there" is positive, isn't "you missed something fantastical".

Although you may wish to attend every event but this isn't possible. However, be patient and don't keep track of your attendance. This could cause them to feel like your friendship is something you have to be able to pass.

If you're the one who isn't able to go to the gym, ensure that you're not postponing it because you don't want to do something. When we want to sit on the couch the mind needs active stimulation. So , go out and have a good time with your pals. It's time wasted.

Chapter 7: E for Effort

"No relationship is accidental."
" O. Henry, Heart of the West

To make your good friends stay with you, you need put in the effort. It's not about providing them with something. It's not about being available at their service. It's the worth of the interactions that will be the most important factor. Planning ahead to incorporate them into your everyday routine is crucial. It doesn't mean you have to be a birthday queen to keep track of everyone's birthday. That's what fridge calendars and phone calendars are made for.

One thing you can create two alarms to mark the birthday of someone on your calendar. One alarm should be set to midnight so that you can write them a message or note message to celebrate their birthday, and another one is to set an reminder of what you're planning to do for them for their birthday.

It doesn't need to be something major. It could even be having a cup of tea after work, or sending them a birthday cake on the day. It is said that thought is important, but it's actually the effort that matters.

If you're the type of person who has a hard time remembering things like birthdays or anniversaries, use technology to aid you. Put it on everything so that you will not forget about it. It should be on your phone calendar as well as your online calendar. It can also be placed on your desk calendar on paper that you keep at work, or at home.

Post-Its are your most trusted friend. Color-code the birthday of your friends from your tribe using your favourite color to ensure that your eyes are drawn to the item when you see it. If you're a kind of person who uses a paper organizer be sure to keep track of every day on it. Include the "week before" note on your planner to ensure that you aren't stressed over what to buy.

If you are aware that you'll have plenty to handle during the quarter, make the group purchase for gifts. This will save you a shopping trip which you'd have to schedule when other things are already taking up your time. If you don't purchase things quickly and you don't rush, you could end up having less expenses than a rush visit to the mall.

Small details can also build up into routine. Make sure you do not only check in on someone every time you have time. Look at what they're doing and make contact early in the early morning. A lot of people will be a little irritated to send bible verses or other quotes so very early in the day. However, make it a consistent practice and they could find themselves looking forward to it.

Do not overlook the simple reality that individuals might not receive any messages from anyone the time of your visit. The simple act of adding them to an email or text message can make a difference to someone's day.

We believe that exerting ourselves takes much energy. However, it is actually an effective way to make us feel more energetic. If we are motivated for our day, the things that we do are intentional rather than routine. Routine can create stress as well. Therefore, make sure you take the time to try something new that could alter your routine. You can create a positive impression on someone else and also take a different approach. This is a win-win-win.

You should be on the lookout for someone willing to become your friend only if you give them something. Leech-like creatures should be removed before they can cause harm.

Don't expect them return the favor. Do not always request anything in return. Just do it for the pleasure of it, since it makes you feel good. Your tribe members aren't obliged to do anything aside from an honest thank for your kindness. It's not to suggest that you shouldn't be apathetic people. What you'll come to realize about true tribe members is that they won't be able to sit in silence until they have paid you back for the blessings you've brought into their lives.

The little things they do, are worth each and every one of them. Sometimes, we expect things from others , and we do not show them we're grateful. Don't put it off. Be sure to thank those you want to acknowledge at precisely the moment you felt grateful.

The delay can lead to miscommunications. When someone would like to help you, they may rethink their decision. Many people dismiss people who seem unkind. Do not let shyness create an issue when it isn't any. It's a habit that develops after a time. It also helps you feel more relaxed because you are aware that you've acknowledged the efforts of other people.

The tribe members aim to take the burden off the shoulders of their tribe mates. If you know someone who just likes to talk about their worries but does not listen to other people, reach them out. Even if someone is in a difficult situation, they could be able to show compassion towards someone else.

Chapter 8: The Treasures of Life

"Close friends are life's most precious treasures. Sometimes, they know us better than we do. They are honest and gentle. help us and help us, and to share our laughs and tears. The presence of their faces reminds us we're never truly in a lonely place."

-- Vincent Van Gogh

After all the time and effort you put into finding people you feel fit to your lifestyle and you have made the effort to maintain them presence in your life What after that?

The answer is straightforward. Life happens next. Whatever life throws at you, you will have these people there to help you. They're the ones to be there for you when trying to create something fresh. The idea of starting something new from scratch can be a daunting task. However, if you have tribe members who will constantly inquire about what you're doing You would be able to count on help.

Some people may appear to not be worth the effort at first. Their worth will not come to light until you've experienced something that's just too difficult for you to take on. They're not the most loud member or the most active person in the group. At times, even the most lively person is unable to inspire tribe members, a steady and quiet assistance is essential.

What happens when a person disappears or is pushed away from you? Are they still part of your circle? Perhaps, but not necessarily. The reason is that their worth is something you attribute to them. If the fact that they are present gives you peace and peace, then they will remain as tribal members. It's nice when elders are part of a larger group. They may not be on the go and making decisions. But when the situation requires a lot of wisdom and quiet determination they are the ones that the majority of people turn to.

If someone disappears from your existence, there's an explanation. The reason may not be something you did. Many people wonder if the reason your friend isn't there anymore is due to something the group or its members of the tribe did. Sometimes, they just want to leave to find themselves. They are figuring out themselves and their motives.

If they can find their goal, then they will discover a way back. If their goal is very different from the tribe of the past don't hold this as a reason to judge them. You're not abandoned, but you are a part of what they are today. Maybe being part of your tribe led them on the journey of self-discovery.

Being member of the tribe isn't compulsory or everlasting. There are those who are likely to lose due to the passing of time and death. It's not caused by only one aspect. However, them moving away or taking another direction isn't always negative.

We cannot stop any member from leaving the group. Don't let the fear of secrets make them feel shackled in the group. Since a person who is determined in abandoning the group but is being forced to stay, will make the group more hostile towards one others. They'll realize how escape only feasible in the event that everything goes down.

It's not something you'd wish for your friends or family members.

Do not categorize your family members and members of your tribe based on their worth or status. Everyone is equal in value. You may have members of your tribe you feel closest to. However, that doesn't mean you should exclude others when you've picked your top choices. Keep in mind that they all will be you "people". If you don't take them seriously and honestly, they'll leave you. This will create unbalance within your life.

Even if there are no physical impact - because they are part of your group - it could cause tension and anxiety. The majority of the time, we don't have the desire to pursue people who have had already left, but the effect of their departure is felt later. If something truly amazing happens, and we aren't able to pinpoint a particular person, the one we are sure would be most happy it's a bit clouded.

The majority of the time, when people create groups, they examine the members who are in their group. If you are forming the group to keep pace with trends and have many friends, you're not creating the correct tribe. You must carefully and slowly complete the tribe you're creating with valuable people. If you are adding people to keep numbers, you'll be left with regrettable encounters.

You can be confident and know that your tribe will endure no matter what. Being confident that you have trustworthy individuals, even if the group is a mere tribe of three people should be sufficient at present. It is still possible to meet new people even if you're part of one or two tribes.

A tribe does not mean that you don't have the chance to make new friends. It's always between people. If you have the opportunity to get acquainted with someone who could be an ideal tribal member, then you could present them to your current core tribe members.

We are always alert for adventure. Whatever you do in creating new friendships keep in mind that you should never close your doors to possibilities.

Our time is not long enough to be able to meet every person in the world. nice people are able to visit us, and at times bad people are allowed to get into our lives. However, we should never abandon people generally because of this.

Chapter 9: #TribeWorld

"Six degree of distancing does not mean that everyone is connected to each other in six steps. It's a sign that a few people are linked to all else within a couple of steps, while all of us are connected to the world by those small number of."

-- Malcolm Gladwell, The Tipping Point The Tipping Point: How Small things can make a big Impact

We live in a society in which connections are made or even initiated by technology. What can this do to aid you in finding your tribe?

It depends on the way you use it.

Sometimes , people who have the potential to join your community are in the far corners on the web. Many people meet their love partners similarly.

How difficult is it to determine their identity and be whether their online profile is exactly the same as who they claim to be? It's not easy. However, time and intimate conversations can be useful in making this choice. A mix of different methods of communication can help you. With the increasing number of applications that permit "live" features that allow for unfiltered conversations similar to those you could have with a person who is located nearby.

Think of all these mediums as windows you can utilize to discuss your life and then share it. The concept of sharing is now a little skewed due to technology. The things we believe we're sending to our contacts is simply something you can be a scrolling down or ignoring. Your feed is monitored and is filtered to focus on items that you will find simple to connect with.

This limits your world perspective and reduces the possibilities of discovering. The best way to approach this is to make sure you are diversified in your beliefs about what is important. In order to be able to look at things that more conservative or liberal friends share and you can engage everyone in a dialogue. Make sure you are open to dialogue even on social media.

This way, all types of people, who could be tribe mates can be able to connect with your profile. This way, the different kinds of people who might become tribe mates can find your.

A channel through which you can post your thoughts is essential in the present time. There are more and more individuals whom we do not agree with are surfacing in our newsfeed.

The most interesting part is that tribes are now thriving using chat rooms and messengers to communicate what's happening in their lives. However, someone who constantly shares their lives constantly could also be a source of discontent for others.

We can't control how other people think of us. Everyone has their own view and opinions. Even if you're just posting photos of the sunset on the beach you visited and some might interpret it as an attempt to prove that you're on vacation for the second time.

Any positive content you share could be misinterpreted by anyone, which is why it's crucial to keep a check on the people you interact with on social media as well as your personal life. Do not let people you don't wish to hear from get the chance to cause a negative impact on your day or memory.

Chapter 10: The Right Time Now

"Always seek out ways to smile and make someone feel good and also to perform some random gestures of compassion throughout your every day life."

" Roy T. Bennet, The Light in the Heart

If you're thinking of starting an organization and are thinking about the best moment to start, it's now. Your comfort zone that you've been living in for a long time must be expanded. Many people find excuses for doing it the next time, but never take the initiative. The time you devote to trying to figure out what you want to accomplish would be a drain on time you have to go to meet people. People meeting can also mean spending the time spent online, but it's certainly not the identical.

It is essential to engage in interactions with your friends and family members to build the quality of your "tribe-dar". The tribe-dar is a feeling that you build over time as strive to increase the number of members of your tribe.

Certain people possess the natural ability to read others. It is because they are attracted to the specifics. They can discern behaviour from the speech patterns and movements of individuals. However, for all of us we must take time to discern whether the people we are meeting at are real or not.

If you are easily discouraged Try seeking assistance. Discuss with your friends the people you have met. It's like having a tribe-wingman woman. If you talk about your feelings regarding someone with someone you trust, you'll be able to determine if you're being too cautious or irrational.

Take the time to be open to chances. A lot of times, the people you trust are just all the same when it comes down to their faith. Don't let that be the case when you are building your tribe. There should be a large number of opportunities offered to people you would like to include in your family.

Be aware that members of tribes aren't supposed to be perfect people. They're people who make mistakes. If it's not a breach of trust or criminal, their forgiveness shouldn't be a huge problem. Giving them your full forgiveness is a decision that you must make.

If you are a grudger, when they do something wrong then you'll raise it. Friendships should not be a breeze every day. They take an effort that takes time to establish. At the end of the day, it might be one minor factor that could cause the relationship to break.

Do not let the cracks become any larger or create more issues than they caused. Resolving issues requires having conversations and checking regularly whether everything is in order. Making time for your friends from your tribe is essential for a healthy relationship. Even if it's only once a year, after returning from a different place Do not make excuses and simply take a trip.

If you're struggling with your tribe members who you have, think about their importance to you. Be courageous when making your choices regarding who you eliminate.

It's a challenge since other members of your tribe are connected. There is a chance of losing the entire group. However, it's your life, it's your tribe, and you need to determine who are your ideal tribemates throughout your life. Do not settle for less than stellar tribe members and choose the most desirable ones for you.

www.ingramcontent.com/pod-product-compliance
Lightning Source LLC
Chambersburg PA
CBHW050403120526
44590CB00015B/1803